FORE-
WORD

I HAVE just had myself a highly entertaining—and profitable— busman's holiday. For I have just finished reading Why You Lose at Bridge, *this very engaging book written by S. J. Simon, Great Britain's foremost Bridge player.*

I have never met Mr. Simon; and yet I feel I know him. Certainly I know the kind of Bridge player he is. And should it ever be my good fortune to play with him as a partner, I would sit down with complete confidence in the success of that partnership. If, on the contrary, I drew him as an opponent, I would watch my step indeed!

Of this I am convinced because I so much admire his approach to the game. There are in these pages such a welter of cool common sense, such a fund of wholesome card philosophy, such a refreshingly original point of view ("Don't play for the best result possible —play for the best possible result") that one would have to be locked in a very high ivory tower indeed not to profit from them.

But this book is more than the expression of a fresh viewpoint. It is sincere.

It may seem strange that I should make an issue of sincerity in a work of a quasi-technical nature. But the unfortunate truth of the matter is that, all too often in the past, there have been those who have brought out books expounding certain doctrines which they wished to sell to the public, not because they felt they were making a valuable contribution to the progress of the game, but because they were sure that the market could absorb their product.

Mr. Simon's attitude is that of a practical player. He is not so much interested in telling you how to improve your technical skill. Rather he aims to show you how you can get the best results using the skill you already possess. Moreover his ideas are presented in such a light and amusing manner that I am sure the casual reader will find the book delightful as well as instructive.

I can't end this introduction without quoting two paragraphs which seem to me to typify his very human attitude toward the game.

"Keep your bidding simple. Approach when you must and take the direct route whenever you can. Never feel compelled to use a convention where it cannot help you, merely because you happen to be playing it. If you know you want to be in a small slam contract but not in a grand slam, bid 'six' direct. Do not bother with the four-five No Trump routine. Why tell the opponents you have four Aces?

"Whether you are aiming at a part score, a game or a slam, the moment you have decided what your contract is to be, BID it. It may not be very spectacular, it may evoke the jeers of those that like to wander around the world to reach a contract that can be reached in a couple of bids; but believe me, it pays. You will lose fewer points during the year if you stop trying to be scientific all the time."

Though the author's avowed purpose here is to tell the average player how to lose less, there isn't the shadow of a doubt in my mind that even the more experienced player, following these precepts, will win more.

CHARLES H. GOREN

Philadelphia, March 1, 1946.

WHY YOU LOSE AT BRIDGE

By S. J. Simon

♠
♥ ♦
♣

July 2, 1997

To Susan

With many pairs of gratitude for your loving care, grooming, and bedtime biscuits

From

Gene Machine

Jet star's Speaking with Nimba

Published by
Devyn Press, Inc.
Louisville, Kentucky

Printed in the United States of America.

Published by
Devyn Press, Inc.
3600 Chamberlain Lane, Suite 230
Louisville, KY 40241
1-800-274-2221

ISBN 0-939460-75-0

CONTENTS

PORTRAIT

You are an average Bridge player.

You have a fair amount of playing ability, which you imagine is greater than it is. A smattering of all the more popular systems. And a pet system of your own which you play whenever you manage to cut one of your favorite partners.

Your bidding is adequate and your defense quite shocking.

You have no ambition to become a master player, but you like to win.

You do not keep accounts and you tell every body that you think you are about all square on the year.

You lie—and you know it.

INTRO-
DUCTION

Why You Lose at Bridge

THERE ARE two primary reasons:
(a) Lack of technical skill.
(b) Losing tactics.

It is not the object of this book to do much about the first. It is probably too late to do much about it anyway. You've been playing Bridge far too long now to start learning how to play your dummy better. You've been making the same mistakes quite happily for years and you've every intention of going on making them. You don't want to know how to make a contract on a "double squeeze, dummy reversal, throw-in." You don't believe there is such an animal.

And quite right, too. I sympathize. Bridge is a game and you play it for pleasure.

You can well afford to leave such highly technical plays to the expert, the would-be aspirant to the first post-war Bridge Championship. Let him enjoy himself with them, together with his despairing psychics, his ever-weakening three bids, and all the advanced arguments for interminable refinements in the carefully complicated systems that made competitive Bridge such a nightmare before the war, and caused Master Players to lie awake nights regretting that they had not played the seven of Spades and won the match instead of the five and lost it.

I know. I've done it.

In any event, it is not lack of technical skill that makes you a loser at Bridge. Bridge Clubs are full of experts making contracts on double squeezes and losing even more money in the course of the year than you do. And deserving to lose it.

It is not the handling of difficult hands that makes the winning player. There aren't enough of them. It is the ability to avoid messing up the easy ones.

The majority of hands are well within the range of the ordinary Bridge player—well within *your* range. Your technical equipment, assuming you do not insist on playing out of your class, is quite good enough to make you a winning player.

But you're not.

I know, of course, that you are an unlucky player, that you never hold a card, that all your big hands backfire, that your finesses are always wrong, and that if there is a mug at the table you always cut him.

I also know that you throw thousands of points out of the window every time you sit down to play.

Thousands!

Not on contracts you might have made or defeated, not on slams you might have bid. But on points thrown away through greed, obstinacy, refusal to believe the obvious, or just sheer carelessness.

Points lost on mistakes that you are quite good enough *not* to make.

It is not my concern here to increase your technical skill. My concern is to tell you how to make the most of such skill as you may possess.

This book will not turn you into a winning player overnight. But it will at least draw your attention to all the simple tactical, mathematical and psychological mistakes which are the reason why you lose. Mistakes, many of which you are quite unaware that you are making.

If you conquer only a fraction of them you will lose a lot less.

The Points You Lose
"Ignoring the Odds"

THIS CHAPTER is a lesson in simple arithmetic.

Before you skip it let me ask you a question.

"Do you double a contract of six Spades holding two Aces?"

If you do, don't skip it.

Because, like the great majority of Bridge players, you are mathematically oblivious.

And while you remain oblivious, you will never win at Bridge.

You will note that I have written "oblivious" rather than "ignorant." You are not mathematically ignorant. The mathematics involved in Contract Bridge are too simple for that. It is only necessary for you to become aware of them.

This chapter is an attempt to make you aware.

Mathematical apathy is one of the most fascinating sidelights on the world of cards. The mathematical factor is predominant in all major card games. All regular card players, no matter how much they may protest they play for pleasure, like to win. And yet the card player who takes the trouble to be aware of the mathematical principles involved in his game is the rare exception—and usually a professional at that. That is why the professional makes his living so easily. It is not his superior skill that brings him the bulk of his profit—it is his superior mathematical awareness.

The supreme example is Poker. Don't let anybody tell you Poker is a game of chance. Poker heads the list of card games of skill; it is not as interesting as Contract Bridge, but the element of chance is smaller.

Ask any professional who plays both. Give him his choice of playing either in weaker company. He will tell you that his percentage of winnings will be much higher at Poker. And if you ask him how much capital he needs to meet the occasional inevitable losses he will ask for less to play Poker than to play Bridge at proportionately the same stakes.

Poker offers him the maximum opportunity to exploit his skill.

And that skill is mainly *mathematical*.

Psychology, bluff, flair, ruthlessness—these things help. But a Poker player may lack them all and still be a winning player as long as his betting remains mathematically correct.

Let me explain why Poker is mainly mathematical. I know that this is a book about Contract Bridge; but it won't do you any harm. And it will help you to grasp the more obscure mathematics of Contract if you already understand the glaringly obvious mathematics of Poker.

I assume you know how Poker is played. There are two betting phases. The first after the deal, the second after players, still in the pot, have bought their cards. After the deal you must decide whether the five cards originally dealt to you warrant the stake you have to expend to remain in the game:

That decision is mainly mathematical.

You must weigh the amount of your stake against the amount you stand to win and compare that, in turn, with your chances of winning it.

Say you hold four to a flush. The chances of buying a fifth card in the same suit are, approximately, 4–1 against you. Assume you decide that it is a good odds-on bet that a flush will be good enough to win this particular pot. Before you pay to play you must be sure that there is enough money already staked to offer you a return of better than 4–1 should you win.

It is obvious that if you keep on accepting less than 4–1 you will win an occasional pot that you might otherwise have missed, but you will be a big loser in the long run. If you only accept over the odds, you will miss an occasional small pot that you might have won, but you are a certain winner in the long run.

Simple—isn't it?

Clearly the same principles apply to all the other combinations and situations at the Poker table.

How much do I risk?

How much can I win?

What are my chances of winning?

And yet, believe it or not, the great majority of Poker players who turn up at their clubs night after night, pay only slight attention to odds. They are nuts on psychology and will tell you that Mrs. Winklestein always fiddles with her diamond ring when she is bluffing. But they are quite unaware what their chances are of making three Aces out of two.

They just buy three cards and hope for the best.

Or, worse still, cut their chances another 33 per cent and buy only two cards in the hope that some timid soul will subsequently believe they started with three of a kind.

Clearly even Mrs. Winklestein cannot bluff often enough to make up for that.

A great game, Poker. I must learn it some time.

Now the three principles I have mentioned for Poker apply just as forcibly to Bridge:

(a) How much can my bid or play gain?

(b) How much can it lose?

(c) What are its chances of success?

And that brings us right back to where we started.

"Do you double a contract of six Spades holding two Aces?"

"I do!"

"Why?"

"Because I think they won't make it."

"How certain are you?"

"Pretty certain. I mean, I've got two Aces. . . . Of course, if one of them should happen to be void. . . . "

"Then they'll redouble, won't they?"

"I couldn't help it. Rotten luck. I had two Aces, partner. I had to double."

Who compelled you?

Stop and work out the odds a minute.

Opponents have bid six Spades—let us say, not vulnerable. You do not anticipate setting them more than one trick. If they go down one undoubled you score 50 points. If they go down one doubled, you score 100 points.

Your prospective gain by doubling is 50 points.

And now let us look at what happens if they make it.

6 Spades undoubled......................180

6 Spades doubled.......................410*

6 Spades redoubled.....................770*

When opponents fail to redouble you stand to gain 50 points and to lose 230. You are laying odds of more than 4–1 on your-

---

*50 points above the line for making a doubled contract.

self. And in these days, with all the slam bidding aids available, two Aces will certainly not defeat a slam contract in a suit more than half the time.

By doubling you are laying 4–1 on an even money chance.

And what happens if the contract is redoubled? You are still laying 4–1 for your gain is now 150 points, but your chances of success, by the mere fact of the redouble, can no longer be ranked at even money. Two to one against you is nearer the mark.

So it boils down to this. Every time you double a slam in a suit simply because you hold two Aces you are laying yourself open to giving odds of 8 to 1.

It can't be worth it.

Vulnerable, your double is slightly less dreadful. You now stand to gain 100 points if it is successful and lose only 180 points if it fails. Or 300 to 540 if redoubled. But against that the overtrick, should they make it, will cost you 200 points (or 400 redoubled). And grand slams have been made against two Aces, particularly when you lead out the wrong one.

It still can't be worth it.

Curiously enough there is a worse crime than doubling a suit slam holding two Aces, and even more curiously, it is indulged in by players who have learned enough to avoid the first excess.

That is the double which enables declarer to make a contract *he might otherwise not have made* by placing the missing high cards.

If you double because you hold two Aces it is not likely that you will present declarer with his contract. If he has to follow suit to both of them he will be one down and that will be that!

But if your double enables the declarer to make a contract he might otherwise not have made, you have handed him not only the extra points of the double, but the value of the game and the slam as well.

And even when your double succeeds, more often than not, you will fail to gain the miserable 50 or 100 points that you have risked so much to secure. For it will be found on analysis that, without the double, declarer would have been two tricks down instead of one.

An example will make this quite clear. I hope.

Sitting East you hold:

♠ : Q J 9 2
♡ : A
◇ : 9 8 7 6 4
♣ : J 5 2

[12]

South is the declarer at a contract of 6 Spades.

On such a holding ninety-nine Bridge players out of a hundred would double without hesitation. The Ace of Hearts looks certain to make; and the trump holding must surely provide at least one trick.

And ninety-nine Bridge players out of a hundred would be wrong.

Even assuming that the bidding precludes the possibility of a successful switch to six No Trump, consider the following possible trump distribution:

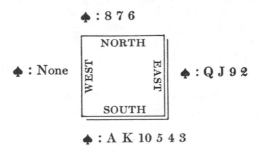

♠ : 8 7 6

♠ : None   ♠ : Q J 9 2

♠ : A K 10 5 4 3

If you refrain from doubling, the contract is certain to go down. Declarer is not likely to play the eight of Spades from dummy on the first round and let it ride. If he does, you should hold your cards up.

His correct play is the Ace of Spades and after that he will go down. Quite possibly, in view of your singleton Ace of Hearts and the number of times he must enter dummy in order to play through your trump holding, two down.

But if you double, he will run the eight of Spades through you and make his contract. Or, at worst, go down one less than he would have undoubled.

Now let us look at the mathematics of your double.

Remember that your double presents the declarer with at least one trick.

6 SPADES DOUBLED		6 SPADES UNDOUBLED		PROFIT	
	Not		*Not*		*Not*
Vul.	*Vul.*	*Vul.*	*Vul.*	*Vul.*	*Vul.*
1 down...200	100	2 down...200	100	Nil	Nil
2 down...500	300	3 down...300	150	200	150
3 down...800	500	4 down...400	200	400	300

So if you defeat the contract two tricks your profit is only 150–200 points. Even if you defeat it three tricks, which is most

[13]

unlikely unless your opponents are lunatics, your gain is only 300–400 points.

And now look at what you lose if the contract is made.

	Not Vulnerable	Vulnerable
Value of small slam.........	500	750
Value of game..............	300	500 (or 700)
6s doubled.................	180	180
Bonus for making doubled contract.................	50	50
6s 1 down undoubled........ (since the contract would probably have gone down if you hadn't doubled).	50	100
Total..................	1080	1580 (or 1780)

So, if your double is successful, your gain averages approximately 250 points; if unsuccessful, your loss averages 1380 points.

Not very good odds, is it? Almost 6 to 1 against the double.

And we have not even taken into consideration the possibility of a redouble or an overtrick.

But maybe you're still not entirely convinced. In the example I've given, you'll argue, declarer will go down most of the time. There is no reason why the A, K, 10 of Spades should be over you—dummy has only to hold one of the honors—or there may be an insufficient number of entries in dummy—you can't expect all the breaks to be against you. You certainly have every right to expect to defeat the contract far more often than seven times out of eight.

I agree with you. You will.

But you have forgotten one point. Your double is almost certain to present declarer with at least one trick.

You have got to set him two to show even a small profit.

And how often will you do that?

So most of the time you are risking all to gain nothing.

I have elected to write about slam doubles because they are the most spectacular as well as the most expensive example of neglected mathematics at Bridge. But clearly the argument applies just as strongly to other phases of the game. However, before I pass on to them, I must, for my own protection, make one other point about doubling slam contracts. Otherwise I shall be accused of advising you never, in any circumstances, to double a slam.

I have done nothing of the kind.

[14]

I have told you not to double a slam because *you think you can defeat it.*

I have no objection to your doubling a slam because you think you cannot defeat it *any other way.* In fact, I insist on it.

There is a big difference between doubling a contract because you think it is going down anyway, and doubling because you hope your double will cause the contract to be defeated. A big mathematical difference.

You may have heard of the Lightner slam double. It was invented, astonishingly enough, by Mr. Lightner, and it calls for the lead of an unexpected suit. In other words, if your partner has bid Hearts and subsequently doubles six Spades, the one lead he does not want is Hearts. He is shrieking for a Club or a Diamond (probably he can ruff one of these suits) and your holding and the opponent's bidding will almost invariably indicate quite plainly which to lead.

To my mind the Lightner slam double ranks as one of the most brilliant contributions to Contract Bridge yet made. It is simple. It is practically foolproof. It prevents partners who play it from making other, idiotic slam doubles. And it is mathematically advantageous. I'll swap you all your Asking Bids for it, and throw in the Blackwood Four-Five No Trump as well.

After what I have just written about not doubling slams the "mathematically advantageous" may appear surprising. It isn't.

I do not mean that the Lightner slam double will defeat a slam all the time, or even necessarily most of the time. For one thing declarer might over-ruff. But I do claim that it will defeat many slams that would not otherwise be defeated. And for that reason it is mathematically advantageous.

See if you can work out why before I tell you.

If you can, you are now mathematically awake and will never fall asleep again.

And now for the answer.

When you double a slam because you think it is going down anyway, you stand to gain between 50–100 points and to lose, as we have seen, rather more than that.

With the Lightner slam double you still stand to lose quite a lot of points. But you no longer stand to gain only 50 points. You stand to gain the value of the game and the slam. *Because otherwise you think the slam will be made.*

And even when the double fails and declarer makes his contract it will hardly ever be your double that gives it to him.

For all practical purposes I might just as well have written "Never." But there is no practical "never" at Bridge, and I

[15]

do not wish to be plagued by the hard luck story of some reader, who was about to find the only lead to defeat a slam contract when his partner Lightner-doubled, so he led a different card and "they made it." Such hands do happen—I could construct one for you easily enough. But they happen too rarely to matter.

So, for all practical purposes, your Lightner-double runs an average risk of presenting opponents with 180 points rising to a maximum of 940 (6 Spades Vul. redoubled, 7 made) and stands to gain around 1000 to 1500 points.

At the worst it is even money. On the average it is about 6 to 1 in your favor.

A considerable difference from doubling on two Aces, isn't it?

It is not in the least necessary for you to have a knowledge of the exact odds involved in the various bids and plays at Contract Bridge. I don't know them all myself. But it helps if you have an approximate idea of the odds involved in all stock situations. And it is absolutely essential to understand the argument behind their calculations.

Let me, like some schoolmaster drumming it into his pupils, revert to my three key questions:

(1) How much can my bid or play gain?
(2) How much can it lose?
(3) What are its chances of success?

Make certain that you are answering them correctly.

Question (3) is straightforward enough. If the chances in any particular case are too difficult for you to work out, ask the nearest mathematician. There is always one handy.

It is in answering the first two questions that so many players go wrong. They think only of the actual result—the figures that will be written down on the score sheet. They do not think of the invisible profit or loss—the figures that do not get written down, but are nevertheless still very much there.

Thus if they bid a non-vulnerable game and go down one, they think of the loss as 50 points written down to the enemy. But the actual loss is 90 points (3 Spades made)+50 (1 down) +50 (value of part score)=190 points.

In the case of an unsuccessful small slam the loss is more obvious because the value of the game is involved as well. But the calculation is exactly the same.

Thus it is obvious, when you are considering any bid or play, that you must know not only what that play stands to gain if it succeeds, but also the total amount it will lose if it fails. It is only by comparing the two that you arrive at the correct odds and can decide whether the play or bid is worth making.

And that brings us straight to the most common fallacy in Contract Bridge—so common that it is practically quoted as an axiom to beginners.

Here it is:

"When vulnerable, bid more cautiously than when not vulnerable because the penalties are greater."

Most Bridge players believe this implicitly and thus prove my point that they are mathematically unconscious.

Because the statement above is only true of defensive bidding —the hands on which you expect to go down.

When you are bidding aggressively, when you are hoping to make your bid, the situation is quite the reverse. Your penalties for failure may be greater than when you are not vulnerable— but your rewards are greater still.

Consider the most common case of all: whether to try for game or take a part score:

Not Vulnerable

Gain

4 Spades bid and made...120+300 for game.   Total 420

3 Spades bid, 4 made.....120 (90 below the line and
                             30 above)+50 (part score value)
                                             Total 170

Net Gain for bidding game   250

Loss

4 Spades bid 3 made.....50+90 (3 Spades made)+50
                        (value of part score)
                                         Total 190

Odds in favor of bidding game 250/190. Or rather better than an even chance.

Vulnerable

Gain

4 Spades bid and made...120+500, or 700 for rubber.
                                    Total 620, or 820

3 Spades bid, 4 made.....As before   170

Net gain for bidding game.450 or 650

Loss

4 Spades bid, 3 made.....100+90 (3 Spades made)+50
                        (part score value)   Total 240

Odds in favor of bidding
    game ....620 or 820/240. Or, from 2-1 to 3-1
                                       in your favor.

So against non-vulnerable opponents who never double, it is worth while bidding a vulnerable game that depends on two finesses, a 3–1 chance against. However, as opponents are always liable to double and, on a 3–1 chance, may get you down more than one, these odds are too high.

But you will still show a good profit on balance if you consistently bid your vulnerable games at odds of 2–1 against you.

Which is considerably higher than the odds that can be accepted with profit for bidding a non-vulnerable game.

So stop telling your partner you thought you'd have a shot at game because you were not vulnerable.

Shoot it when you are.

And that, I think, is all I need to say about the mathematics of Contract. I can see no reason for working out with you further examples of the application of odds to other bids and plays. I have only done it in this instance, not because I thought you were incapable of working them out for yourself, but because I was pretty certain it had not occurred to you to do it.

I only wanted to make you aware of their existence.

CHAPTER

TWO

The Points You Lose
Playing the Dummy

How DO you play your dummies?

Let me paint a picture.

Even if you deny that you play like that, you will certainly know someone else who does.

Or, on second thought, let us call the declarer Mr. Smug.

Because, for some reason which I have never discovered, you are sensitive about your dummy play. You admit that your bidding may not be up-to-date, and your defense could be better, but give you a few good cards and you'll play them with anybody. And in the next breath you disclaim all knowledge of the more advanced plays—you can't be bothered with them.

Which makes this a delicate chapter to write.

I don't want to hurt your feelings.

And I want to talk about some of the plays which you have always considered too advanced and prove that they are not so advanced at that and practically no bother.

Anyway, let us get back to Mr. Smug.

Mr. Smug, sitting South, has just dealt himself the following hand vulnerable:—

♠ : A J 9 4 3 2
♡ : A 4 2
◇ : 5 4
♣ : A 7

For once the auction proceeds smoothly, and Mr. Smug finds himself in a contract of four Spades. On the bidding Mr. Smug can see little reason to anticipate any difficulty. In fact he is wondering mildly whether he has missed a slam. West had hesitated slightly before passing, but, of course, Mr. Smug has not noticed that.

West leads the King of Diamonds and dummy starts to put down his cards.

The Ace of Diamonds!

"Put the Ace on," orders Mr. Smug, without even waiting to see the complete dummy.

Dummy proves as follows:—

♠ : K 8 6
♡ : K J 10
◇ : A 8 7
♣ : K J 10 9

Mr. Smug inspects it. If he can guess both the Club and Heart finesses right, he will make a grand slam.

"Probably missed it, partner," he announces.

You will note that it has not even occurred to him that he might lose a trump trick.

Mr. Smug now decides he might as well get this rather boring hand over with quickly. He plays the King of Spades from dummy.

East discards a Heart.

Mr. Smug chuckles.

"Well, well," he says. "Lucky we kept out of it, partner."

His partner looks at him.

Mr. Smug draws another round of trumps. He looks at the dummy again and his expression gets a little worried. It has just occurred to him that the contract might go down. He has only to take a finesse wrong and he has four losers. But presently he brightens. He has found a way of giving himself an extra chance and he is very proud of it.

If he plays the Ace of Clubs, followed by the King of Clubs, and trumps the third round, the Queen of Clubs might fall. Then all he need lose is two trumps and possibly a Heart.

Well played, Sir!

So Mr. Smug plays three rounds of Clubs, trumping the third. But West over-trumps, cashes his winning trump, cashes a winning Diamond, and plays another Diamond. East discards a second Heart.

And here is Mr. Smug reduced to a successful Heart finesse to make his contract.

Mr. Smug now goes into an agonizing trance. It is not quite

[20]

clear what he is thinking about, for at the end of it he cashes the Ace of Hearts and leads a small Heart towards dummy.

West shows out and that is that.

"Can't help it, partner," says Mr. Smug. "Everything was wrong."

And he is blissfully unaware that the hand is cold for five odd.

Are you?

Not that I suggest you would play the dummy quite as badly as Mr. Smug has played it. He has managed to include in it practically every mistake a declarer can make. But I do suggest that the mistakes he has compressed into this one hand you are spreading quite happily over many hands.

Let us enumerate Mr. Smug's mistakes:

1. Hasty play to first trick.
2. Mismanagement of trumps.
3. Failure to throw a loser on a loser.
4. Failure to count the hand.

* * * * *

Before we return to the correct play of Mr. Smug's dummy, I would like to discuss these four types of mistakes individually. They are, all four of them, very common mistakes. You will agree about Nos. 1 and 2, but you may claim that Nos. 3 and 4 are less mistakes than advanced plays too complex for you to bother with. But I hope I can show you that counting a hand, or throwing a loser on a loser, is not necessarily a feat accessible only to experts. Quite a lot of the time anybody can do it.

Let us consider the mistakes in order.

1. HASTY PLAY TO FIRST TRICK!

This is perhaps the most common fault in Contract. Too many other Bridge players have stressed it already for me to emphasize its importance. In any case, you are perfectly well aware of it yourself—you have lost far too many contracts by doing it not to be.

But I can try and cure you.

You have often tried to cure yourself, but you have not succeeded. You remember part of the time, but you cannot remember all the time.

The reason is simple. You cannot cure a symptom. For your tendency to play quickly to the first trick is but a part of the whole haze of optimism that surrounds your dummy play.

[21]

How often have you started off playing a hand in a crescendo of confidence and dwindled down to a series of agonizing trances each longer than the last?

Let me try and replace your habit of hurried early play by another habit. It is clearly too much to ask you all at once to survey the whole situation, envisage possible snags, and plan your campaign before playing to the *first* trick. You will have to get into the habit gradually. And the first and most important step in that direction is comparatively simple.

Never win a trick until you have made up your mind what card you are going to play next.

This applies even more strongly to defensive play. We shall deal with that later.

No matter how obvious the card you have to play, do not play it immediately—not even when it is a singleton in the suit led. Stop and decide on your next play before you make the present one.

And if you protest that you dislike trancing, let me point out that the recommended process takes no longer than your present one. If you take the trick at once you have still to think of the next play before you make it. If you have thought of it before taking the trick you can make it at once. It adds up to the same.

The habit of mentally planning the next trick before winning the present one is about the most useful habit a Bridge player can form. For one thing, it automatically prevents the hasty play we are discussing. For another, the mere mental process of thinking what to play next may induce you to change the card you were about to play. And finally, having got into the habit of embarking on this train of thought, you will often find yourself fascinated into continuing it and thus achieve the complete survey of the hand that I hesitated to impose upon you earlier in this chapter.

Next time you find yourself at the same table with the club professional, study his technique. Note how he compresses his thinking. A trance at the start of the hand as dummy goes down. Another trance after a few tricks to assess the information gained. A third trance, if the hand is difficult, to decide his squeeze or end play. And the smooth culmination. Note that the only time you see him trancing after winning a trick is when he has won it unexpectedly; on the other occasions he has completed his trancing before he wins it and the next trick follows immediately.

But now watch Mr. Smug towards the end of a sticky hand. A trick is offered him—a dubious gift. He trances. He takes it. He trances again. . . .

In spite of all the years you have misspent playing your obvious cards quickly, merely because they were obvious, I do not think you will find it too difficult to think one trick in advance. Especially if you refrain from fingering any card until you have decided to play it. Particularly an obvious card.

And once you have acquired the habit you will never play too quickly to the first trick again.

2. MISMANAGEMENT OF TRUMPS

You have heard of safety plays. There are quite a few Bridge players, most of them would-be master players, who would be quite a lot richer if they had never heard of them.

At Bridge a little knowledge is at least twice as dangerous.

That is why, to digress on a pet aversion of my own, I roar, rant, tear my plentiful hair, and spit blood at the spectacle of theory-saturated palookas, fitted only to play a "one club" system, following in the doubtful footsteps of their super-scientific masters and indulging in orgies of asking bids, protective bids, shaded suit responses, or reverses with no suit at all.

When a Master Player elects to open "one Spade" holding ♠ : 10, 8, 7, 6, it may or may not be poor strategy—a case can be made either way. But when a palooka does it, it is sheer impertinence. And a clear case of trying to run before he can walk.

Enough of the scientist for the moment. We shall meet him again later, when I will try and tell you how to cope with the pest. But there is really very little one can do—except cut against him.

In safety plays, too, there is the danger of becoming too scientific.

My object in this discourse is both to draw your attention to the merits of safety plays and, at the same time, warn you against allowing them to become an obsession. Overindulgence is just as bad as complete neglect.

A safety play is, in its essence, an insurance policy. A small premium, in the form of a trick that need not necessarily be lost, is given up to insure against a far greater loss.

The simplest example is the contract of three No Trump, with dummy holding a six-card suit headed by Ace, King, and no entry and declarer holding three small cards of the suit. Here even a beginner knows enough to duck the first round in the suit. If the remaining cards in the suit are divided 2-2, he has lost a trick—that is his premium. But if they are divided 3-1, the duck enables the whole suit to be run.

[23]

From this baby example we go into the whole range of safety plays. The simpler ones you probably know already; the more ingenious ones may have escaped your attention. I do not propose to list them here—it would savor too much of homework and in any case it is far more satisfying to work them out for yourself at the card table as the need arises.

But make certain first that the need is really present.

For that is the danger.

Players who have just discovered safety plays are apt to be so proud of their knowledge that they miss no opportunity of displaying it—irrespective of whether the situation permits such a luxury. For it is a luxury. It means letting the enemy in. And you must be very certain that the damage they might do with the extra tempo is, in fact, less than the danger you are guarding against. If, in our above contract of three No Trump, the player sitting over the six-card suit in dummy has established a suit of his own, it is no longer a safety play to duck the first round of the six-card suit into his hand. It is plain lunacy.

Of course, you still insure cashing your six-card suit—*after the opponents have taken their tricks!*

But the danger is not always quite so apparent, which is why you so often here a shame-faced declarer, who has gone down in a stone-cold contract, announcing pathetically, "I played it for safety, partner."

I have even heard it in an international match.

In Room 1, North-South bid six Spades and made five. In Room 2, North-South stopped at 4 Spades and declarer, playing for safety, made three.

No swing!

On another occasion I watched an international player, notorious for his pessimistic outlook on distribution, playing a hand to guard against the five outstanding trumps being held by one opponent. He played it beautifully—had all the five outstanding trumps been in one hand he would have made his contract. Unfortunately, they were divided 3-2, so he went down one. Unlucky!

Here, from actual play, is an example of the type of pitfall lurking for the safety player.

The hand:

♠ : K 6
♡ : 5 4 3
◊ : K Q J 5
♣ : A J 9 4

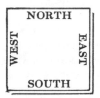

♠ : A J 9 7 5 4
♡ : A K Q J
◊ : A 6
♣ : 5

The bidding, with enemy silent throughout, has gone:

SOUTH	NORTH
2 ♠	3 NT
4 ♡	4 ♠
6 ♠	

West leads the Heart 10. All follow and declarer wins with the Ace. He plays the King of Spades and all follow. He plays a small Spade from dummy and East follows.

What card would you, as declarer, play now?

On the face of it the finesse seems marked. The contract looks safe provided you do not lose more than one trump trick. So you appear to have the perfect safety play of the Jack of Spades. If West holds the Queen he can make it and welcome—you will draw the remaining trump and spread your hand.

At any rate, that is what the declarer, who played the actual hand, thought. He took the finesse. West won with the Queen and played a second Heart, which East trumped. Down one.

Now, to my mind, the declarer was wrong. It is true that his play guarded against losing two tricks in trumps. But, in taking it, he was exposing himself to a far greater danger—the danger of a ruff. West had elected to open a suit bid by the enemy. He must have had a reason. He may have been playing safe, by refusing to open an unbid suit, but it was clearly more probable that he was trying to give his partner a ruff. And at any rate, the danger was much greater than finding four trumps in one hand.

In this case I have some sympathy for the declarer.

[25]

The danger was not outstandingly apparent. Still, he ought to have foreseen it. It was myself, by the way.

It seems as though my treatise on safety plays is mainly concerned with warning you against them. And so it is. I want you to be certain that when you do make a safety play it is, in fact, a safety play for the hand as a whole, and not just for one phase of it, and a menace to the rest.

It is not the doubtful contracts that call for safety plays. Doubtful contracts need a spot of luck in the distribution for their fulfillment. And the safety play is a guard against unlucky distributions.

It is on the contracts that appear cast iron that the safety play should be remembered.

3. FAILURE TO THROW A LOSER ON A LOSER

This play consists of playing a loser from one hand and throwing on it a loser from the other—to the enemy's disadvantage. It is usually considered an advanced play. So it is —part of the time. Some of the more spectacular examples are as difficult as anything there is in Bridge and certainly beyond the scope of this book to illustrate.

But most of the time the play can be ridiculously simple. In fact, there are several loser-on-loser plays that you are in the habit of making yourself, without it occurring to you to call them by such an impressive name.

Every time you fail to ruff an enemy card for fear of an over-ruff, and throw away a loser instead, you are making a loser-on-loser play. Just as you are when you have led the twelfth card of a suit towards dummy and, finding it covered on your left, do not ruff for fear of an over-ruff but discard one of dummy's losers and eventually ruff that suit instead.

Now you have only to grasp this principle you are using already to find immediately that you can extend it a great deal further.

If the loser you are playing from one hand is promoting a winner in it, you can discard *two* losers from the other hand.

For instance:

♠ : 6 5
♡ : K Q 6 4
◇ : K Q 5
♣ : Q 10 7 6

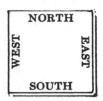

♠ : A J 7
♡ : None
◇ : A J 10 9 8 7
♣ : A K J 9

The contract is six Diamonds by South. West leads the Club two.

Now the obvious play for the contract is to give up a Spade trick and ruff the third Spade.

But this line of play is not 100 per cent safe. You can only afford to take one round of trumps before giving up the Spade trick. If you take two rounds of trumps and the trumps are divided 3–1, when you give up the Spade trick, the remaining enemy trump will be played, killing the chance to ruff the third Spade. And if you only take one round of trumps—well, the Club may be a singleton.

However, there is an absolutely safe way of playing the hand, regardless of any distribution, even four trumps in one hand. A loser-on-loser play.

Win the first trick with the Ace of Clubs.

Draw trumps. Enter dummy with the ten of Clubs. Play the King of Hearts and throw a Spade on it. The Queen of Hearts will now take care of your remaining Spade.

Elementary. It has only to occur to you to do it. And there are masses of hands offering this type of play.

Equally elementary is the loser-on-loser end play:

♠ : K J 6 5 4
♡ : Q 4
◊ : 5 4 3
♣ : K Q 6

♠ : A Q 10 9 8 3 2
♡ : None
◊ : A Q 8
♣ : A J 10

Contract six Spades by South. West leads the King of Hearts.

At first sight the contract appears to depend on a Diamond finesse. But only at first sight. Because a second look reveals an absolute baby loser-on-loser end play.

On the lead West is marked with the Ace of Hearts.

Trump the King of Hearts, draw the trumps and take three rounds of Clubs ending in dummy.

Play the Queen of Hearts and throw the eight of Diamonds on it. West wins with the Ace of Hearts, but now must lead a Diamond, giving you a free finesse, or else a Club or a Heart, either of which permits you to ruff in dummy and discard the Queen of Diamonds from your own hand.

It couldn't be easier.

Even if dummy instead of the Queen of Hearts holds the Jack of Hearts the play is still worth trying. West may hold the three top honors in Hearts, or East may hold the Queen and omit to cover the Jack. And even if East puts the Queen up you have lost nothing. You can still fall back on the Diamond finesse.

I repeat that all loser-on-loser plays are not as easy as this. But the really difficult ones are rare, while the ones that are well within your grasp are happening all the time.

4. FAILURE TO COUNT THE HAND

Now don't be frightened of this one. The only reason that you regard counting a hand as one of those unfathomable mysteries available only to experts is that you have never attempted to count one.

[28]

It is evidence of the aura of mystery that surrounds the counting of a hand that Bridge beginners are liable at any moment to inquire in appropriately awed tones, "I suppose after a few rounds you can tell every card in everybody's hand."

I cannot.

A Master Player is not a species of magician gifted with supernatural powers denied to the rabble. He is merely a person who has mastered the principles of Bridge and can apply them rather better than you can. He cannot work miracles. If you double him in a grand slam holding the Ace of Trumps he will go down.

Yet I have seen a master player (Harrison Gray) left undoubled in precisely this situation. (Yes, even master players can get into such contracts.) Further, to make quite certain that the grand slam did go down, the dear old lady holding the Ace of Trumps led it. Questioned on her failure to double she seemed surprised.

"You don't know Mr. Gray," she said. "He always redoubles."

I cannot tell you what cards every player holds after a few rounds. Most of the time I have not the least idea of all the cards anybody held even after the entire hand has been played out. Sometimes, when the hand calls for it, I can make a fairly accurate assessment of opponents' holding. And occasionally the count of a hand is thrust upon me.

And I never have to do anything more difficult than to add up to thirteen.

Let us go into this thing from first principles.

There are fifty-two cards in the pack. When dummy goes down declarer can see twenty-six of them.

There are four suits and thirteen cards in each suit.

Adding the totals of each suit in both hands and subtracting from thirteen gives the total number of cards in each suit held by the enemy.

All that remains to find out is how they are distributed in the two hands.

And the information for this comes rolling in as the hand progresses.

Let us take a very simple example.

♠ : Q 10 9
♡ : A Q 5 4 3
◇ : Q J 6
♣ : J 5

♠ : A K J 8 7 6
♡ : 7 6
◇ : 10 9 4
♣ : A 4

The contract is four Spades by South. West leads the King and Ace of Diamonds. East follows to the first round, discards a Club on the second round, and trumps the third round. He now leads a Club, which you win with the Ace.

You have lost three tricks. Your contract therefore depends on your Heart finesse being successful and setting up the Heart suit for a Club discard.

You play the Ace of Spades. West discards a Diamond. You now finesse the Heart Queen. It wins. You play the Ace of Hearts and West drops the King. You play a third Heart and trump it. West discards a Diamond.

You now enter dummy with a trump, West discarding another Diamond. A fourth Heart is trumped, the Queen of Spades draws East's last trump and the long Heart is a discard for the losing Club.

Not a very difficult hand to play, calling only for a certain amount of timing. And at no time the count of the enemy's hand. As long as the Heart finesse was right and the Hearts not worse than 4-2 that was all that mattered.

You are right. The count is of no use to you on this hand, as it will be of no use to you on very many other hands. But as this is such an easy count I propose to count it with you—just to demonstrate how it's done.

We begin this hand with no knowledge at all of the distribution. The second trick, when East discards on the King of Diamonds, gives us our first information. West holds six Diamonds and East one.

[30]

We play a round of trumps and now know all about the Spade suit. West none—East four.

The third round of Hearts gives the Heart suit. West two, East four.

The count is now complete.

West no Spades, two Hearts, six Diamonds and therefore five Clubs.

East four Spades, four Hearts, one Diamond, four Clubs.

The underbidders! Fancy not sacrificing in five Clubs. Only down one and not vulnerable at that.

I have purposely chosen a hand on which getting the count is of no value. There are a great many such hands. And there are a great many more on which contracts are made without getting a count, though getting the count would have made making the contract a certainty. They explain the apathy towards hand counting in the Bridge world.

One can get along quite nicely without it.

But there are also a great many hands that might be made without getting a count by fortunate finesses, but where getting the count would make the contract a certainty. If you are getting along nicely, you will fail to guess right half the time. And that costs you quite a lot of points during the year.

For that is the value of hand counting. It helps to reduce the number of times you have to say, "Sorry, partner, wrong guess."

In all those cases where you are faced with a choice of a two-way finesse, or finesse or drop, or, if your dummy play is advanced enough, finesse or squeeze—the count, if you can get it, is a great help. Often it will turn the guess into a certainty. But in any event it will almost invariably indicate which course offers the better chance.

Say you are faced with a two-way Queen finesse in Clubs. Without a count it is even money which way you take it. But say you get the count and find the opposing Clubs divided five and two. It is now five to two that the Queen of Clubs is with the hand holding the five Clubs. It will not always be in that hand, but you will be right more often playing it that way.

Of course, getting the count is not always quite as simple as in the example I have given you. In that hand it was just handed to you. But there are quite a lot of cases where you can set about finding out for yourself.

Here is a simple but neat example:

♠ : J x
♡ : A K x x
◇ : x x x
♣ : K J x x

♠ : A K Q 10 x
♡ : x x
◇ : x x x
♣ : A 10 9

The contract is four Spades and West leads the Queen of Hearts.

Assuming everything normal, the contract clearly depends on placing the Queen of Clubs correctly.

On this hand the majority of declarers would draw trumps, take a chance on the Club finesse; and, if they guessed right, hope for an overtrick. They would guess right half the time.

But this is the perfect hand for messing about in the hope of something turning up to convert your even money guess into an odds-on chance, or even a certainty. The perfect hand on which to try and get a count. Even if you fail entirely you are not much worse off than those other declarers—you can still guess right half the time about the finesse. And the most your messing about can cost you is an occasional extra trick down —a small price to pay for your added chance of making the contract.

Here is the manner in which you should mess about:

Win with the Ace of Hearts and draw trumps, which, let us assume, break 3–3. Now play the King of Hearts, followed by a third round of Hearts and throw a losing Diamond on it. If either opponent shows out you have a count on the Heart suit. Assume they both follow and West wins the trick.

To your surprise West now goes into a trance. A moment's thought will tell you what he is thinking about. Your Diamond discard has given him the impression that you are maneuvering for a Club or Diamond lead and he is trying to guess which. So clearly he does not hold the thirteenth Heart.

[32]

Note that straight away you have given yourself an extra chance of making the contract—the chance of the defense going wrong. As West almost certainly holds a high honor in Diamonds he is on the spot, and he will guess wrong half the time.

But let us assume he guesses right and leads a Diamond—the King. East signals with a high Diamond. West beams and leads the Jack of Diamonds. East wins with Ace.

If East is a good player he will now play his long Heart rather than another Diamond in an attempt to stop you getting the count. But it does not matter which he plays as you have got the count anyway. West's play of the King of Diamonds followed by the Jack has told you all you wanted to know. If he had held K, J, x he would have led the small Diamond, and if K, Q, J he would have opened the suit; or, in any event, not have tranced when he won the third round of Hearts. Therefore, his Diamond holding is K, J alone. Therefore East holds five Diamonds.

The count on the hand is now complete.

East three Spades, four Hearts, five Diamonds, one Club.

West three Spades, three Hearts, two Diamonds, five Clubs.

The contract is now certain.

Play the Ace of Clubs and if East does not drop the Queen, annoy the opponents by spreading your hand, announcing the Club finesse through West.

One final comment. When I first learned how to count a hand I was so thrilled with my ability that I used to practice it by trying to get the count on every hand I played, irrespective of whether it was going to do me any good on the hand or not. This, of course, produced a number of unnecessary trances and held up the game and annoyed opponents—who wanted to know what the hell I was trancing about. It is probable that the same thing will happen to you. But it doesn't matter. The novelty of counting a hand just for the fun of it soon wears off. Presently you will be using your new and very useful weapon instinctively only when it is required.

And now we can return to the hand **Mr. Smug** messed up.
Remember it?

♠ : K 8 6
♡ : K J 10
◇ : A 8 7
♣ : K J 10 9

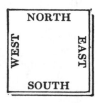

♠ : A J 9 4 3 2
♡ : A 4 2
◇ : 5 4
♣ : A 7

Contract four Spades. King of Diamonds led.

You will remember how Mr. Smug played the hand.

He put up the Ace of Diamonds without waiting to see the rest of the dummy. Having seen it he announced that he had probably missed a slam.

He played the King of Spades from dummy and East discarded a Heart.

He played the Ace of Spades. He cashed two rounds of Clubs and trumped a third round, hoping the Queen of Clubs might drop. But West overtrumped, cashed his winning trump, cashed his winning Diamond, and led a third Diamond. East discarded A SECOND HEART.

And Mr. Smug was reduced to a successful Heart finesse for his contract.

He played out the Ace of Hearts and led a small Heart towards dummy. West showed out and that was that.

"Can't help it," said Mr. Smug. "Everything was wrong."

Let us now examine his four errors and their effects:

1. HASTY PLAY TO FIRST TRICK

The error is unpardonable, but in this case it cost nothing. The Ace of Diamonds happens to be the correct card to play. Mr. Smug could not possibly have been aware of this. for he did not even wait to see the whole dummy before making the play. He was just lucky. Or possibly the author just couldn't manage to construct a hand in which this error could be penalized without disturbing the balance of penalties awarded to all the subsequent errors.

2. MISMANAGEMENT OF TRUMPS

The error here is one that a great many players, including non-concentrating experts, would make. In rubber Bridge particularly one is apt to treat apparently easy hands with undue optimism and make light-hearted plays from which it is difficult to recover later. It is not that the expert doesn't know the safety play on these occasions. It is just that he feels he cannot be bothered to work it out. After all, the four trumps have got to be in one hand against him—and they probably aren't.

But in this case they are.

And there is a perfect safety play available for not losing more than one trick.

♠ : K 8 6

♠ : A J 9 4 3 2

Try and work it out for yourself.

If you cannot, here is the answer.

Play over to the Ace of Spades. Now if there are four trumps in either hand, they can be picked up with the loss of one trick only.

3. LOSER ON LOSER

Mr. Smug has missed a sitter.

Instead of trumping the third round of Clubs and lamenting that the Queen of Clubs had failed to drop, he should have allowed the Jack of Clubs to run, throwing his losing Diamond on it.

One of two things would now happen.

(1) West would win with the Queen—in which case dummy's ten of Clubs is a discard for the losing Heart.

(2) East has failed to cover, and West must now either follow with a small Club or use one of his winning trumps.

In either case the contract is safe.

[35]

4. COUNTING THE HAND

In spite of all Mr. Smug's mistakes the contract is still on ice. There is no need to guess the Heart finesse. A complete count on the hand became available when East failed to follow to the third round of Diamonds.

Let us trace it.

At trick 2 East was found to be void in Spades. This marked West with four Spades.

At trick 6 West overtrumped the third round of Clubs, marking him with two Clubs only.

At trick 9 East failed to follow to the third round of Diamonds. This marked West with six Diamonds.

West's hand is marked with six Diamonds, four Spades, two Clubs, and therefore ONLY ONE HEART.

The play is marked. A small Heart towards dummy, and when the Queen of Hearts does not appear from West, put up the King. Now play the Jack, and let it ride.

Counting a hand will help you to retrieve many situations that you have messed up earlier.

And now I want to stop talking about the points you lose as declarer and concentrate for a moment on the points you might win by tempting the defense to do your work for you.

Making life difficult for the defense is one of the most satisfying aspects of dummy play. There is little satisfaction, though quite a lot of profit, when the defense throws a contract at you. But if you have planned the manner in which they shall throw it, what a contentment in leaning back in your chair and arbitrating their recriminations!

The really ecstatic hands, the hands in which you put in an opponent to squeeze a seething partner, do not happen often. But simpler opportunities are occurring all the time, mainly with regard to the trump suit.

Take the following trump holding—when you can afford to lose only one trick:

♠ : Q 5

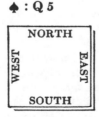

♠ : K 10 9 8 7

Without the help of the defense, or other indication, you have to rely on making the right guess of the trump division. But if you can persuade the enemy to lead trumps for you. . . .

The best and most often available means of persuasion is to suggest that you are trying for ruffs in dummy. Often you will be holding a doubleton in the same suit in both hands. It can never hurt to lead it. It often comes off. And if by chance you hold a singleton in dummy which is of no value to you, then the play is almost certain of success.

As in the following hand I played recently:

♠ : A J 10 7 6
♡ : 3
◇ : 10 6 5 4 3 2
♣ : 7

♠ : 2
♡ : A J 10 9 8 7 6
◇ : A 8
♣ : K Q J

Bidding (North & South Vulnerable):

SOUTH	WEST	NORTH	EAST
1 ♡	1 ♠	Double	Pass
4 ♡	Pass	Pass	Pass

West led King of Spades, which I won with Ace; North had not failed to conceal his displeasure of my take-out of his double, which would certainly have been calamitous for East-West, so I was not too happy on viewing the dummy. Prospects of going down were quite good. To avoid it I had to lose only one trump trick. And even if the trumps were divided to make this possible, how should I play them? Finesse the Jack on the first round and trust East had a doubleton honor? Or try to drop the King, Queen blank? It was so easy to make the wrong guess.

Fortunately, there was another alternative. The singleton Club offered a first-rate deceptive play. The bidding made it odds-on that West held the Ace of Clubs, and when he had won the trick with it he would be on the spot. And even if the play failed, I still had the chance of dropping the King, Queen of Hearts blank.

So I played the Club and put up the King. West won, and after a heart-breaking trance led the Queen of Hearts from Q, x.

It will be seen that any trump play by me would have failed.

This hand is not nearly such an ample pat on my back as I have made it appear. The play stands out the moment you have thought of it. And that is just the point. Get into the habit of looking for these opportunities and you will be delighted to find how many of them there are.

Finally, I should like to offer a suggestion for dealing with those constantly recurring situations facing the declarer, such as the two-way finesse, the combined holding of nine trumps missing the Queen, and others of the same type.

When there is no other indication, and only when, I suggest that you make yourself a few set rules for dealing with them. At the moment you are probably making up your mind each time. Quite a lot of mental strain is being wasted, for in my opinion (unless, of course, you fancy yourself a good guesser) it will get you no better results than the rule of thumb. And if, as judging by their conversation most Bridge players seem to do, you *never* guess right, you will be considerably better off.

It does not matter much what rule of thumb you adopt, provided there is a reasonable mathematical basis for it.

For instance, this is the rule I have made for myself for playing a combined holding of nine trumps missing the Queen.

First play the Ace or King to see what happens—if nothing happens, proceed as follows:—

With *no* singletons or voids in your hand or dummy, play for the drop.

With a singleton or void in either hand, take the finesse.

I believe myself that this gives me a slight advantage; for it is based on the Culbertson Theory of Similarity of Distributions, which argues that when there is a singleton in one hand there will be a compensating singleton elsewhere.

But even if I show no profit, I certainly show no loss—and I haven't got a headache each time I come up against the situation.

If you prefer to play for the drop all the time, or finesse all the time, you won't be very far wrong either. The chances of each are about even. But if you guess every time and you are not very lucky in your guesses. . . . .

[38]

Similarly there is that unmitigated nuisance—the two-way finesse for the Queen. Having exhausted all other alternatives I play for the *Queen to lie over the Jack*.

There is an argument that there is an advantage in playing it this way. It is based, not on mathematics, but on the imperfect shuffling of the previous deal, when the Queen in question may have covered a Jack.

Whether there is anything in this theory or not, it is at any rate an even money chance, which is all your guess is. And at least it saves the headache of guessing every time.

CHAPTER

THREE

The Points You Lose

in Defense

I SHUDDER to think of the total number of points you throw away in defense every year. For that matter I shudder at the total number of points I throw away myself.

I do not mean by this that my defense is as bad as yours. It is, almost certainly, much better. But it is still a long way from being good.

Defense is difficult. Much more difficult than dummy play. Good dummy players exist in reasonable abundance; but the really good defensive player is a very rare animal—even among experts. In the whole of Great Britain (and I think I have played with every expert, or near expert, in it) I know only three who, in my opinion, can claim this honor. To name them would bring a storm about my ears. So I won't.

Richard Lederer was a fourth.

As for the majority of master players the kindest description of their defense is the word "adequate."

The reason why defense is so much more difficult than dummy play is obvious. A declarer knows the exact strength that is massed against him. A defender doesn't. Like the declarer, he can see twenty-six cards once dummy is down, but all that he knows about the other twenty-six is that his partner has thirteen of them. The rest he has to work out for himself.

And, as though this were not enough, he has to make the opening lead without seeing the dummy.

The dice are loaded in favor of the declarer.

From time to time there has been talk of a change in the laws.

It has been suggested that dummy should be exposed before the opening lead. I am against this. It would practically annihilate all chances of getting away with impossible contracts based on bluff or psychological bids. And they are half the fun of the game. But I am inclined to think it would be fairer. There is very little fun and no fairness in having to find a "blind" opening lead against a bluff contract that probably would be routed if you guess right, and made with overtricks if you guess wrong. There may be retribution—but that is a personal matter.

To become the perfect defensive player at Bridge you will need a combination of logic and flair. You must be sound or brilliant as the occasion demands. You must be able to draw the right inference from the bidding, visualize all the possibilities, and grasp what declarer is trying to do, often before he attempts to do it, in order to select the most promising lead. On top of this you still need perfect partnership co-operation.

Which makes the whole thing impossible.

So this chapter does not set out to teach you how to break apparently cast-iron contracts. Its ambition is much more limited. It hopes only to reduce the number of unmakable contracts you allow declarer to make.

Here, to my mind, are the three major causes of Gifts to the Declarer:

1. Premature winning of tricks.
2. Getting busy at the wrong moment.
3. Informative trancing.

1. PREMATURE WINNING OF TRICKS

It is likely that you already realize something of the importance of refusing to win a trick at a moment that suits the declarer. For instance, when dummy has a long suit with no entry you know enough to hold up the Ace of that suit until declarer can no longer bring it in. Or, sitting with a King over an Ace, Queen, Jack suit in a No Trump contract, to hold off for one round.

But do you carry the principle any further?

For instance, if dummy, armed with plentiful trumps, plays a singleton through your Ace—do you always play your Ace?

If you do, you will be wrong most of the time.

To make this point clear, consider this situation:

Declarer leads a small card that might be a singleton towards, say, K, Q, x, x, in dummy. Sitting second hand, holding the Ace of that suit, do you always hop up with it?

Of course you don't. About the only time you play your

Ace in such a case is when you believe you can immediately cash sufficient tricks to set the contract. And the reason that you hold off most of the time is that even if declarer's card *is* a singleton, your play of the Ace will give him two discards later.

The principle is exactly the same when a singleton is led *from* dummy.

Let us take a hand and study it both ways:

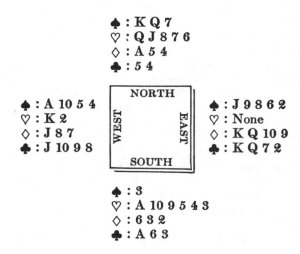

♠ : K Q 7
♡ : Q J 8 7 6
◇ : A 5 4
♣ : 5 4

♠ : A 10 5 4   ♠ : J 9 8 6 2
♡ : K 2   ♡ : None
◇ : J 8 7   ◇ : K Q 10 9
♣ : J 10 9 8   ♣ : K Q 7 2

NORTH
WEST   EAST
SOUTH

♠ : 3
♡ : A 10 9 5 4 3
◇ : 6 3 2
♣ : A 6 3

The contract is four Hearts by South. You have led the Jack of Clubs, dummy has played the five, your partner the Queen, and declarer has won with Ace. Declarer now lays down the Ace of Hearts, looks annoyed, and leads a Spade towards dummy.

Clearly you cannot even contemplate playing the Ace. If you do so, even if the Spade is a singleton, declarer will discard two losing Diamonds, if he has them, on the King, Queen of Spades. And if he hasn't two losers in Diamonds the contract is unbeatable. So you duck with your Ace and declarer loses no tricks in Spades—but now he must lose two Diamonds as well as a Club and a Heart, and is down one.

Played this way the hand seems so elementary that you may be impatient at the amount of time I am wasting on it.

But consider it the other way round. Assume the Auction has gone differently—that North is the declarer and South the dummy. East now leads the King of Clubs, which dummy wins with the Ace.

North plays the Ace of Hearts, looks annoyed, and leads the singleton Spade from dummy. And there you are.

[42]

It is exactly the same situation as before—down to the last card that I have so carefully constructed. If you put up the Ace, declarer will make his contract. If you duck he will be down one.

And yet the majority of defenders, who would automatically duck in the first instance, will just as automatically put up their Ace in the second.

Remember, as a further argument in favor of ducking, that the concealed hand need not necessarily hold the King, Queen of the suit led. It may hold the K, J, in which case, if you fail to put up the Ace, declarer, reasoning from what he would do himself, will almost certainly finesse the Jack. Or it may hold Q, J, 10, in which case your partner's King will be picked up on the second round and a discard achieved later.

I have been a confirmed ducker of Aces for many years; and the number of cases in which it has lost me a contract or even a trick are very few. It will not always yield two tricks in return, but at any rate the ducked trick almost invariably comes back.

So start ducking with your Aces. But do not consider yourself graduated until you have successfully ducked with an Ace in such a position as to defeat a small slam contract.

Here is the supreme test of courage. Opponents have reached a contract of six Spades, declarer having bid Hearts originally. Dummy goes down with a singleton Heart; and you, sitting over the dummy, hold ♡ A, J, 5, 4. The singleton is led.

Duck like a man!

Put up the Ace and one ruff will probably establish declarer's Hearts; duck and he'll have to ruff three times.

It may disorganize him completely. And even if he still survives, you will nearly always get your trick back from somewhere else.

Of all the Aces that I have ducked against slams I can only remember one where my ducking presented opponents with the contract. And then it was only because they had reached the slam missing two Aces. My partner quite failed to appreciate the essential soundness of my play!

That is why I say it requires courage.

There is another instance of ducking that is insufficiently practiced—the duck to gain a tempo. For example, sitting with A, J, x over a suit K, Q, x, x, x, it often pays to refuse the first round. Win the first trick and declarer with a doubleton can ruff out the suit without disturbing dummy's entry. Duck, and he can't.

There are many equally obvious instances where this play gains, and many more involving end-plays and squeezes, which are not quite so obvious. And even if you are not up to squeezes

[43]

and end plays yourself, you have no guarantee that the declarer isn't.

So whenever you are convinced that such a duck can be no harm and might do some good, make it.

Another "frequently missed" duck, centers around the scientific sounding "Principle of Promotion." It occurs when you are in a position to over-ruff declarer and, by refusing to do so, gain an extra trick. The simplest example—not often missed by the way—occurs when you hold A, J alone in trumps and declarer ruffs with the King. If you over-ruff, his Queen will now draw your Jack. If you refuse to do so you must make two trump tricks.

But alter the trump holding a little—make it A, 10, x, and it is surprising how many defenders will blissfully over-ruff declarer's King when by not trumping at all they must take two tricks against declarer's original King, Queen, Jack.

Or make the trump holding A, 8, x—is there any reason why you should not try to promote the eight? After all, your partner might hold the nine and the ten.

I always remember with pleasure a hand where on precisely this holding (Spades A, 8, x) I collected two trump tricks against declarer's "hundred honors partner!" to set the contract. We had taken one trick when my partner led a Heart, of which I was now void. The declarer ruffed with the ten and I ducked. Declarer led King of Spades, which I *won with the Ace*, my partner dropping the nine. This left me with 8, x over his Queen, Jack. I now led a Diamond. Partner, bless him, won with the Ace and led another Heart. Declarer had to use one of his trump honors to shut me out, thereby promoting my 8 into becoming a winner.

2. GETTING BUSY AT THE WRONG MOMENT

The second source of Gifts to Declarer, "Getting Busy at the Wrong Moment," is not nearly so clear cut, and it will be difficult to find satisfactory examples of what I mean, though actual examples are happening in their thousands at the Bridge table daily. So I propose rather to talk about the principle.

There are two main types of defense at Bridge:
   (a) Busy
   (b) Passive
The busy defense is when you endeavor to develop your own tricks before the declarer can develop his.

Passive defense is when you play every card safe, refuse to open fresh suits, and leave the declarer to do all the work for himself.

[44]

That is the crux of the whole matter.

A great many contracts are chucked at declarer by getting busy instead of staying passive, or staying passive instead of getting busy. Accordingly the chief problem a defender has to decide upon is whether to get busy or stay passive.

Unfortunately he nearly always gets busy.

It is not entirely his fault. Most of the Bridge literature written about defense has been written about busy defense. There has been so much learned illustration of competing tempos—so much written about beating the declarer to the punch by setting up your own suit first—that the defender's state of mind is one of feverish urgency—a burning desire to do something, try something, anything rather than sit still and let declarer get on with it. Practically the only thing the student has absorbed of passive defense is a disinclination to lead away from tenaces—and, at that he usually remembers it at the wrong moment.

And yet as many contracts (particularly No Trump contracts) are defeated by passive defense as by getting busy.

So the question to ask yourself when deciding whether to get busy or stay passive is:

Can the declarer, if left in peace, develop enough tricks to make his contract?

If he can, get busy.

If he can't, stay passive.

Getting busy involves taking risks. But if you know that by staying passive declarer will make his contract, it is obviously necessary to take the risk, and get busy. If, for example, there is a suit in dummy that can be set up for discards, then clearly you must attempt to get at your tricks before the suit can be set up. If your getting busy gives him overtricks—that's neither here nor there.

But if there is no long suit in dummy, if there appear to be no tricks declarer can develop that he hasn't got anyway, don't help him. Stay passive. Don't open up new suits for him. Left in peace he might well go down.

But, and it is a big but, how are you to diagnose whether the declarer needs time to develop tricks? Never mind cases where there are long suits or potential ruffs in dummy—you can diagnose these easily enough—what about those hands where the menace isn't so apparent? How are you to tell if there is danger or there isn't?

Well, the answer is that you can't. You can only judge each case on its merits and go by probabilities. Say, for example, after a few tricks have been played you find yourself on lead against a four Spade contract. Trumps have been drawn and dummy contains nothing of interest except four Clubs to the Jack, 10. There has been nothing in the play as yet to show whether the declarer's side strength is in Clubs or Diamonds.

Is the Club situation a menace? Should you attack Diamonds, in which you hold an honor, or punch declarer with a Heart and let him get on with it?

Your own Club holding gives you the answer. If you hold two or three small Clubs there is clearly no danger. Whatever tricks declarer has in Clubs he will make. You can punch him with a Heart safely.

But if you have four little Clubs it is not so good. If declarer, for example, holds A, K, x, he will drop your partner's Queen and get a discard. Or if he holds A, Q, x, he can play the Ace followed by the Queen and your partner cannot hold off. And it may be too late then to attack the Diamonds. The same applies if you yourself hold a doubleton to an honor in Clubs. Clearly in these last cases you have to guess declarer's Club holding. Personally, I usually stay passive anyway—but then I'm a lazy person.

But where it pays most to be passive is in No Trump contracts where declarer and dummy have strength in every suit, but no particular length in any of them. Time and again, as the declarer in such a contract, I have started out with about six certain tricks and a number of hopes and have ended up making a comfortable four No Trump, owing to the defense's frantic efforts to find holes in my armor, attacking every suit in turn and so giving me finesses I might have guessed wrong if I had been left to take them for myself. Think back to the No Trump contracts you have played yourself. How many have been chucked at you in this way?

And how many have you yourself chucked?

I have a very set rule in this matter. The moment it's clear that this is going to be a close contract, with the declarer groping for his tricks (and often this can be told from the bidding) I go passive. I make a neutral lead, something like the ten from 10, 9, x, and allow declarer to find his own way. Every time he puts me on lead I get off it by playing a card in one of his certain tricks.

Let him sweat.

Here is an example:

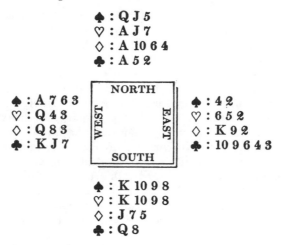

♠ : Q J 5
♡ : A J 7
◇ : A 10 6 4
♣ : A 5 2

♠ : A 7 6 3
♡ : Q 4 3
◇ : Q 8 3
♣ : K J 7

NORTH
WEST   EAST
SOUTH

♠ : 4 2
♡ : 6 5 2
◇ : K 9 2
♣ : 10 9 6 4 3

♠ : K 10 9 8
♡ : K 10 9 8
◇ : J 7 5
♣ : Q 8

The contract is three No Trump by South. You are West and lead a small Spade. Declarer wins with the Queen of Spades in dummy and leads the Jack of Spades on which you hold off, as it can do you no harm and a discard from your partner might prove illuminating. Declarer leads a third Spade. Your partner discards a small Club.

There is now no doubt about the matter. This is a passive hand. Your partner has not signaled in any suit. Let declarer find his own tricks—you are not going to do a thing to help him.

So win the third Spade and get off lead by playing another Spade. Your partner, if he is wise, will refuse to give the declarer any clues to the Heart suit, and will discard a second Club.

On the fourth Spade dummy has to find a discard. The only safe one is a Diamond. So good-by to declarer's hope of establishing that suit.

Declarer now takes the Heart finesse. For the sake of this example he takes it wrong—into your hand.

GET OFF PLAY WITH A HEART.

And the declarer is still left guessing.

Note that from the beginning declarer had eight sure tricks —three Spades, three Hearts, one Diamond and one Club.

If you return anything except a Spade at the fourth trick you present him with his contract.

By staying passive you give him a chance to go wrong.

3. THE INFORMATIVE TRANCE

The third source of Gifts to Declarer is the vaguest of all. But, against an alert declarer, it probably costs you more than the other two put together. I mean the Informative Trance which helps declarer to place the cards.

It may still be useful to refuse to win a King with an Ace, but it loses a great deal of its value if you trance for half an hour before refusing. It may not always be advisable to cover an honor with an honor. But when you don't, for heaven's sake don't hesitate. And when you refuse the finesse declarer has taken towards your King, refuse nonchalantly and smack your partner's hand if he has dared to stretch it across the table. And finally, if you get into trouble over your discards while declarer is playing out his long suit, don't let him see it. If you are forced to blank a King—look happy about it. Don't let your anguished wriggles tell declarer you've got it. He might not know.

And it is no use arguing that declarer is an unethical cad to take advantage of your distress. It is considered quite ethical for declarer to take advantage of your demeanor, so why should it be considered unethical to put on a demeanor to bluff declarer?

Personally I hold the revolutionary view that Bridge would be a much fairer game if it was played all-out, with every kind of vocal intonation or expressive gesture considered in order and absolutely sporting (though not stacking the deck or indulging in physical violence, like kicking your partner under the table). There is so much unconscious and unavoidable cheating anyway—every pair that plays together continually just can't help cheating through their knowledge of each other—that it would be far more ethical to abolish all ethics.

Perhaps I'm not serious. Or am I?

Anyway, I do not propose to argue the point here. If I started I should never stop, and I might tie everybody into knots, including myself. So let's leave it at that.

It is perfectly ethical for declarer to draw inferences from your hesitations. But you must not hesitate purposefully in order to fool him.

Therefore you must learn to stop hesitating.

Now, it is impossible to stop hesitating all the time. There are too many situations in Bridge where you are taken by surprise and simply have to stop and think.

So do your thinking in advance.

Most of the trancing situations in defense can be seen coming long before they arrive. The moment you see them, stop and

[48]

decide what you will do. Then by the time the declarer makes the play, you will be ready for him and give nothing away.

Take that famous example—your Ace over a singleton in dummy. It is apparent the moment dummy goes down that sooner or later declarer will lead that singleton. Make up your mind what you are going to do before it happens.

There are usually plenty of opportunities for thinking inconspicuously. Few declarers play like lightning. And while declarer is trancing—you can get your own trancing done.

If declarer is disobliging enough not to give you an opportunity, you can still find time for your trance before the critical moment by doing it during another trick altogether, though preferably avoiding one when you have a singleton of the suit led. For instance, when declarer starts playing out all his trumps, don't discard happily and wait to trance until you are in difficulties. Take your trance while you are still happy, work out what is going to happen and what you are going to do about it. Then, if you decide you must leave yourself with a blank King you will at least avoid that final trance that tells declarer what you have done.

OPENING LEADS

Defense is the most difficult part of Contract Bridge. And opening leads are the most difficult part of the defense.

For this reason I propose to say little about them in this book. The standard opening leads are too elementary to need discussion here, and the higher strategy too advanced. Too advanced for me, anyway.

We, in England, never realized how much we had to learn about opening leads until Dr. Stern's Austrian team, who had beaten the Culbertsons to win the International Championship of Europe paid us a visit to trounce a scratch English team in a friendly match. What impressed us was not their bidding (we still think ours rather better), nor their dummy play (which was excellent, though no better than some of ours), but their defense. And particularly their opening leads. "Devastating" was the word unanimously used by players and spectators to describe them.

Have you, in your eulogics of the Bridge players you consider good, ever described their opening leads as "devastating"? It is probably the one aspect of their play that has not come up for discussion.

I have only two suggestions to offer you on opening leads. Neither of them is devastating, but they will save you many points during the year:

[49]

(1) (*a*) Whenever your opponents have bid three suits and ended up in a fourth;

(*b*) Whenever declarer, supported in his suit, has bid No Trump and been put back into his suit again;

(*c*) Whenever you haven't the faintest idea what to lead—

Lead a trump.

The reason is obvious. In the first two cases, dummy has ruffing values and the sooner you attack trumps the better.

In the third case, it is the lead that is least likely to do any harm.

(2) When you are in doubt whether to open your partner's suit or your own—

Lead your partner's.

If you lead your partner's suit and discover later that a lead of your own suit would have set the contract—it is unlucky and that's all there is to it. And if you feel like it, you can bawl out your partner for making weak overcalls.

But if you lead your own suit and find partner's suit would have set the contract, your partner is not likely to be pleased.

Personally I use this argument in all cases where the decision is close. I prefer the position where I can bawl out to one where I can be bawled out, whether I like it or not.

Mathematically, the choice advocated may not save many points on the hand in question. Psychologically, it shows a handsome profit on subsequent hands. The gain comes from the improved temper of partner.

CHAPTER

FOUR

The Points You Lose
"Bidding"

As THE reader may have inferred I hold some very positive views about bidding. And while this chapter is in no way concerned with swaying you from the system you happen to favor, this does not seem to me to be a reason for concealing my contempt for some of them. If at the end of it you are converted from playing some particular brand of scientific nonsense imbibed from experts who ought to know better, I'm delighted. If not—that's fine too. I only hope I cut against you some time.

And so I'm going to open this chapter with a warning against that super-scientific but insidious poison that is oozing out of a group of perverted experts to infect masses of well-intentioned, eager-to-learn players—turning them from honest straightforward bidders that it is a pleasure to play with into muddleheaded idiots lost in a nightmare of undigested, misapplied and, in the main, unsound theory.

The weak three bid on Q, x, x, x, x, x and a bust! The shaded suit opening on four to the umpti! The reverse bid on two four-card suits merely for the sake of reversing! The super-strong butt-in demanding better values than an opening bid! The trap pass! Its miserable corollary, the protection bid!

It is possible that the poison has not reached your circle. It will. When it does, ignore the convincing scientific patter that accompanies it. Study the results the infected players achieve. That's all I ask. *Study their results.*

Let there be no confusion. I am not running down scientific bidding. I am running down super-scientific gibberish.

[51]

Some hands at Bridge demand delicate treatment, others are best dealt with poppa-momma fashion. Reserve your science for the hands that need them. Do not get scientific on every hand merely for the sake of science.

For that is just what the super-scientists do. They are striving for an accuracy of bidding that does not exist in Bridge and, in striving for it, they turn the simplest hands into problems. They have to bid twice as well to achieve the same results as a normal pair. And they don't achieve it.

I shall always remember with pleasure an inquiry addressed to Harrison Gray and myself by one of these super-scientific pairs at the half-time interval during a duplicate match. How, they inquired, puzzled, had we managed to reach three No Trump on Board No. 14. There were nine cold tricks in high cards, but they had taken five rounds of bidding to get into four Hearts and go down two.

Neither Gray nor I had any recollection of the board. However, obligingly, we hunted out the bidding slips. We found we had bid this difficult hand as follows:

North, 1 No Trump.
South, 3 No Trump.

If these scientists kept their ideas to themselves, it would not be so bad. At least they understand what they are trying to do and why. But they *will* teach others!

It may be all right for the super-scientist to open one Spade on:

♠ : 9 8 7 6
♡ : A K Q J
◇ : A 5 4
♣ : A 2

I am liable to do it myself if the mood seizes me. But if I do it, I am experimenting and am fully prepared to apologize profusely if it goes wrong.

But the super-scientist will teach the eager student that one Spade is the *only* correct bid on the hand, and that an opening bid of one Heart is out of order. If you open one Heart, he explains patiently, you will never be able to bid your Spades. And the palooka listens agog to find himself a few hands later playing four Spades doubled with seven trumps between the hands.*

*Followers of this system will please refrain from writing in to point out that, as partner is not allowed to give first round support to a suit without four trumps, such a contract is impossible.
Because it still seems to happen.

Such teaching is not merely bad Bridge. It's cruelty to Bridge players.

Let me implore you, for the benefit of your pocket and your partner's temper, to keep your bidding as simple as you can. Aim at using the minimum rather than the maximum number of bids to reach your contract. The fewer the bids the fewer the opportunities to make mistakes. Follow the principle laid down by my ex-partner, M. Harrison Gray, adopted gratefully by me, and jeered at as dull and uninspired by scientific and scintillating pairs, who invariably finished miles below us in any pairs tournament:

"Bid What You Think You Can Make"

This still permits you to be as scientific as is necessary on the hands that demand it. You can approach, reverse, ask, bid four No Trump and produce the whole bag of tricks as it is required. But not when it isn't. The moment you know the declaration you want to play at, you bid it without any further nonsense.

For example, if partner bids one Club and you hold

♠ : x
♡ : A K J x x x x
◇ : x x
♣ : x x x

You think you can make four Hearts. Do not bother with a beautiful approach bid of one Heart. Bid four Hearts directly. Never mind about missing a slam. In the first place it probably isn't there; in the second place there is nothing to prevent your partner making a slam try over your bid. And, finally, if your partner does not make a try, and you miss the slam, your bid will still show a bid profit in the long run. For, if you make a beautiful approach bid of one Heart, the most probable result is not that you will miss a slam, but that the enemy will sacrifice at four Spades.

The fewer your bids, the fewer chances you give your opponents to get together. Thus, if you hold a little better than a double raise in Spades, bid three Spades or four Spades according to mood and partner. Don't dally with some mark-time bid of two Clubs on some fatuous Club holding, and give opponents a chance to get together. What can it gain you? Even if they remain silent, all you have achieved is to present them gratis with some information for defending the hand.

That was the chief fault of the famous "Asking Bids," now happily becoming extinct, at any rate in England. By the time the asking was over, opponents knew the exact weakness of the hand.

Even in slam bidding it is not safe to make unnecessary bids. Admitted, the level is usually too high for opponents to start bidding, but it can happen, as witness the following;—

♠ : 10 9 7 6 5 4 3
♡ : 5 4 3 2
◇ : 2
♣ : 4

I held the above hand sitting East. Both sides were vulnerable, and South was the dealer. The bidding proceeded as follows:—

SOUTH	WEST	NORTH	EAST
1 ♡	Pass	3 ♡	Pass
4 ◇	Pass	5 ◇	Pass
5 ♠	Double	6 ♡	6 ♠!
Double	Pass	Pass	Pass

There was nothing particularly clever about my bid; in fact, the moment partner doubled five Spades it stood out a mile. Hearts had been bid and supported, and I held four of them, so partner was marked with a singleton at most. So what could I lose? Three singletons and, at the outside, two trump tricks; 1100 at the most to save a vulnerable small slam. And it might cost a lot less than that.

Actually it cost a mere 200, for the four hands were:

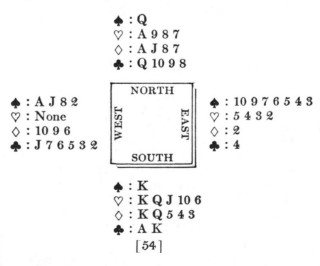

♠ : Q
♡ : A 9 8 7
◇ : A J 8 7
♣ : Q 10 9 8

♠ : A J 8 2
♡ : None
◇ : 10 9 6
♣ : J 7 6 5 3 2

NORTH
WEST
EAST
SOUTH

♠ : 10 9 7 6 5 4 3
♡ : 5 4 3 2
◇ : 2
♣ : 4

♠ : K
♡ : K Q J 10 6
◇ : K Q 5 4 3
♣ : A K

[54]

Best defense can set the contract two tricks, but South led the Ace of Clubs and I was able to set up the Club suit.

However, South's 5 Spade bid was criminal. They were playing the Culbertson Four-Five No Trump, and North had *failed* to bid four N.T. over four Diamonds to show three Aces. So what the devil was South trying to do? Stop a Spade lead and make an overtrick!

Keep your bidding simple. Approach when you must and take the direct route whenever you can. Never feel compelled to use a convention where it cannot help you, merely because you happen to be playing it. If you know you want to be in a small slam contract but not in a grand slam, bid "six" directly. Don't bother with the four-five No Trump routine. Why tell your opponents how many aces you have?

Whether you are aiming at a part score, a game, or a slam, the moment you have decided what your contract is to be—BID IT. It may not be very spectacular, it may evoke the jeers of those who like to wander round the world to reach a contract that can be reached in a couple of bids; but, believe me, it pays. You will lose many fewer points during the year if you stop trying to be "scientific" all the time.

That, at least, is my emphatic opinion. You can accept it, investigate it, or ignore it for it is only an opinion; and there are may who disagree with it.

Now let us proceed to a less debatable discussion of the average player's bidding faults. Here, to my mind, are the most common:

    (a) No Trump bidding.
    (b) Bidding misfit hands.
    (c) Over bidding of big hands.
    (d) Underbidding of small hands.
    (e) Competitive bidding.

(a) NO TRUMP BIDDING

There is an enormous amount of almost abysmal ignorance concerning the structure of successful No Trump bidding. Many players seem to think that it is only necessary to hold a singleton in partner's suit to jump immediately into a No Trump contract. At whatever level the strength of their hand may indicate. For example, holding:

♠ : 8
♡ : A K 6 4
◇ : A 7 5 2
♣ : Q J 10 4

they automatically bid three No Trump over their partner's opening bid of one Spade. And while it is possible that three No Trump may prove to be the eventual best contract on the hand, the bid may, at this stage, easily turn out to be the worst. There is no reason why there should not be a slam in a suit and equally there is no reason why three No Trump should make.

So this is not one of those cases where you jump directly to the contract you wish to be in, for you do not yet know what that contract should be.

The argument used by the "three No Trump" bidders on this hand runs something as follows:—

"I hold Hearts, Diamonds, and Clubs. My partner has bid Spades. What can I lose?"

But, unfortunately, it takes more than a stopper in each suit to make nine tricks. You have to establish at least some of the suits. And a singleton in the opposite hand does not make it any easier.

Imagine, for example, that your partner holds:

♠ : A K J 5 4
♡ : Q 8 3 2
◇ : 6 3
♣ : K 5

This is a perfectly normal bid of one Spade and it should not occur to the opener to disturb partner's bid of three No Trump. But three No Trump may not be made, whereas four Hearts is almost certainly cold. You might even make six.

Take another simple example. Imagine you hold:

♠ : A K J 5 4
♡ : 5 4 3
◇ : A Q 10 3
♣ : 2

You bid one Spade. Partner responds two Clubs. You bid two Diamonds. Partner two Hearts.

You are now tempted to bid three No Trump. You hold all the four suits.

But stop for a moment, picture partner's probable hand, and

[56]

try and count up how you can get nine tricks. Partner has shown nine cards in two suits. This does not leave him many cards with which to help establish yours. And you cannot help him at all.

To my mind the right bid on the hand at this stage is PASS. By now I would consider hopes of game on this hand pretty slim and two Hearts seems as good a spot as any to stay in. But as this will evoke roars of rage from all the people who consider a change of suit forcing, no matter at what time it occurs, it is perhaps wiser to make the next weakest bid—two Spades. As an outsize in optimism I might chance two No Trump. But three No Trump is quite unthinkable.

Give partner the following holding:

♠ : 6
♡ : A 10 9 8
♢ : 8 6 5
♣ : A K J 6 5

Partner's bidding has been conservative. He might well, on your own argument, have bid three No Trump over two Diamonds, but all he bid was two Hearts. Perhaps he didn't like his misfit. But now if you bid two No Trump, he will certainly bid three No Trump and redouble if you are doubled in the bargain. And what are your prospects?

If every finesse in sight is right you might just scramble home; but if the cards lie badly, and opponents defend well, just imagine what can happen! You might not make more than six tricks.

And remember, I have given partner an absolute maximum. He would still have bid two Hearts without the King of Clubs.

But now let us change your hand a little. We will keep the same high cards, but we will alter their location:

♠ : A K 7 5 4
♡ : J
♢ : A 10 5 4
♣ : Q 4 2

You have exactly the same high cards as before; Two Aces, one King, one Queen, one Jack. What a difference! Now you are quite in order to bid three No Trump. If partner has the same hand as before, you have nine tricks in top cards. Even take away his King of Clubs and you still have a first-rate play for the contract.

[57]

Reflect on this. Invent other hands and study them for yourself. You will soon be convinced that something in your partner's suit is needed to help you make three No Trump.

There are 40 points in a pack of cards, counting Ace 4, King 3, Queen 2, Jack 1. With a perfect fit in each other's suits, you may achieve three No Trump with as little as 23 points in the combined hands. With no fit you will find yourself going down on as many as 27 or even 28.

The moment you have understood the importance of "fit" in No Trump, an important corollary follows immediately. It is that a jump response in No Trump shows a certain measure of tolerance, if not actual support, for the original suit bid by partner.

Partner opens one Spade on:

♠ : A Q 9 7 6 4
♡ : A x x x
◇ : x x
♣ : x

and you respond with two No Trump.

Now if your Spade holding is liable to be a singleton and you are bidding No Trump merely because you hold the other three suits, your partner is in a shocking mess. He doesn't know what to do. For if your hand has no fit in Spades, his hand is not worth very much and any further bid may lead to disaster. But if he knows that your Spade holding is, at the worst, a doubleton and probably as good as J, x, x, or K, x, x, he can bid four Spades with utter confidence.

(b) BIDDING MISFIT HANDS

This is where even master players come unstuck. You know the sort of thing I mean. You pick up a lovely looking hand (about 14 points, nice distribution—6, 5, 1, 1), but partner keeps on bidding the two suits in which you have singletons; and before you know where you are, you are out of your depth and doubled for a resounding penalty.

Or, again, you pick up quite a nice looking hand, about 12 points with a void in Hearts. Partner bids one Heart. You respond, say, one Spade. Partner bids two Hearts. You feel your hand is too good, you must make another effort. You bid three Diamonds. It is doubled on your left. Partner bids three Hearts. That is doubled. What do you do now? Bid three No Trump? Four Clubs?

[58]

Fortunately there is a golden rule to be followed for these super-misfits. Even more fortunately it is a very simple rule. It is simply this:

The moment there is a balance of evidence to show the hand is a complete misfit, *stop bidding*.

Never mind if the contract you are in at that moment is clearly a bad contract. If you bid again, you may make it better, but you are much more likely to make it a lot worse. In the real disasters over misfits, it is seldom the first double that would have turned out to be so expensive. It is the final double coming at the end of the partnership's wild rescuing.

I do not deny that occasionally you may eventually stagger into some bearable contract on the hand, but it won't be very often.

Take the following hand:

> ♠ : K 10 x x x
> ♡ : None
> ◇ : K Q x x
> ♣ : K 10 x x

Partner bids one Heart. You respond one Spade. Partner bids two Hearts. I suggest you pass. Admittedly you have a strong hand but where are you going on it? Partner clearly does not hold a good four card minor suit else he would have bid it. He has failed to support Spades.

It is, of course, easy to construct hands for partner to hold on which you will make three No Trump. For instance:

> ♠ : Q x
> ♡ : J 10 9 8 7
> ◇ : A x x
> ♣ : A Q x

If both minor suits break, three No Trump will be in.

But how often will partner oblige by holding such a hand? He is far more likely to hold something like:

> ♠ : x x
> ♡ : A K J x x x
> ◇ : x x x
> ♣ : A x

[59]

or worse still:

♠ : A
♡ : A Q x x x x x
◇ : x x
♣ : x x x

Pass 2 Hearts and you will almost certainly make the contract or go down for a small undoubled penalty. Attempt to improve it and anything may happen, including partner jumping into four Hearts.

Even in those cases where two Hearts is doubled, you should still pass. You have enough high cards elsewhere to keep the penalty low, or even to give partner a chance to make his contract.

In duplicate Bridge, especially in short matches, this safety first policy may have to be tempered. But in rubber Bridge, to my mind, there can be no argument. And remember when you have stopped bidding a misfit, there is always a chance that the enemy may be tempted to protect and find a contract of their own and then you are in a position to sock any such attempt good and hard.

(c) OVER-BIDDING OF BIG HANDS

(d) UNDER-BIDDING OF SMALL HANDS

I am treating these two together for they are to a large extent complementary and often cancel each other out. This is just as well.

The average player overbids his big hands and underbids his small ones. When the two hands are opposite each other this cancels out and a normal result is attained, so the loss on balance is not so large as it might be. Which is the reason for its continuance. On the cancelled hands, both overbidder and underbidder remain oblivious of their errors, while the others are dismissed as unlucky or pass unnoticed.

The trouble occurs when a collection of Aces and Kings goes to the hand of any but a very experienced holder. The ordinary holder, after he has finished gloating over them, will announce his strength with his opening bid of, say, two Clubs. And, if he gets a positive response from his partner, he promptly forgets what he has announced and keeps on re-bidding the same values. Fortunately the opposite hand will usually underbid and so adjust matters. But when that hand is so weak that it cannot underbid; or, more rarely, its owner believes his partner and bids the full value, then the loss is very large indeed.

[60]

Consider the following:

♠ : A K x
♡ : A 10 x
◇ : A K x x
♣ : K Q J

A nice hand, a very nice hand! Not quite nice enough to guarantee game if partner has a complete Yarborough, but nearly nice enough. Still the risk of opening with a forcing bid has to be taken. There are too many holdings on which partner will pass a non-forcing opening but which will, at any rate, offer a play for game. So an opening forcing bid of "two Clubs" on this hand is quite in order.

But, and this is the point so many players forget, once they have bid two Clubs, they have bid the *full value* of the hand. Any further initiative must be left to partner. Assume your partner has done the unexpected and produced a positive response. Assume he has bid two No Trump. All your hand is worth now is a simple bid of three No Trump because you have already bid two Clubs. When you bid three No Trump your partner knows that you have a balanced hand with a count of 23-25 points and he is able to judge exactly what to do.

But what happens in practice? How often does the owner of the two Club hand in this situation bid a simple three No Trump and leave the next move to his partner? The customary spectacle is a deep huddle followed by an inanity ranging from four No Trump to six No Trump. Or else a scientific approach with an equally inane bid of three Diamonds, because he has already decided he is not going to stop under a small slam and is fishing for a grand slam.

But suppose that partner's response has been made on a balanced minimum. Say he holds:

♠ : x x x x
♡ : K x x
◇ : x x x
♣ : A x x

What is going to happen? Assuming a favorable lead and everything breaking favorably, the maximum on the hand is five No Trump. If everything breaks badly you will make exactly three No Trump.

But unfortunately, partner seldom has the minimum. Fate usually seems to arrange that there shall be an extra Queen

[61]

or even King in the small hand, and that makes all the difference.

It is, of course, the possessor of the extra King who should be doing the slamming after his partner has opened two Clubs, not the two Club bidder. But, as a rule, he merely sits there smugly while his partner hurricanes the bidding into a small slam. And it never seems to enter his head that on the bidding, his hand is good enough to bid seven.

It is remarkable how hard it is to persuade the owner of a bad hand, viewed solo, that, placed alongside partner's bidding, it is not merely a good hand, but a whale of a good hand. He continues to view it solo. "What did I have?" he will ask later as partner remonstrates. "Less than a trick and a half."

The example below cropped up just after I had started on this chapter:

♠ : K Q J 7 6
♡ : 8 7 3
◇ : J
♣ : K Q 9 8

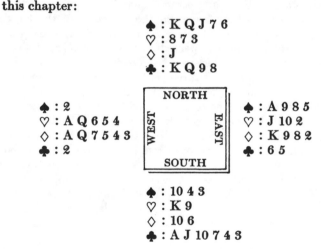

♠ : 2
♡ : A Q 6 5 4
◇ : A Q 7 5 4 3
♣ : 2

NORTH
WEST   EAST
SOUTH

♠ : A 9 8 5
♡ : J 10 2
◇ : K 9 8 2
♣ : 6 5

♠ : 10 4 3
♡ : K 9
◇ : 10 6
♣ : A J 10 7 4 3

I sat West. We were vulnerable. North dealt and the bidding proceeded as follows:

NORTH	EAST	SOUTH	WEST
1 ♠	Pass	2 ♣	3 ♣!
4 ♣	Pass!	5 ♣	Pass
Pass	Pass!!		

We set the contract two tricks, undoubled—a filthy result—as we could have made a small slam in hearts or diamonds. An onlooker shook his head dubiously. In my place, he intimated, he would have bid five Diamonds over five Clubs. After all, he pointed out, if that was doubled, I could always try five Hearts. And up to a point he was right. That is the way the majority of players would have bid the hand. You've got to take some risk, they would argue. Partner must have something! And in this case the majority would have been right and achieved a far less shameful result on the hand than I did. Partner did have something. In fact, on the bidding, partner had a whale of a hand. On his hand, I would have been making a slam try.

Reflect on his hand for a minute. Our opponents had bid Spades and Clubs. So by bidding three Clubs, I had shown a two suiter in Hearts and Diamonds. And he holds K, 9, 8, 2 in one suit, and J, 10, x in the other. In addition he holds the Ace of Spades. His hand could hardly fit better if I had stacked the deck. And yet he passed throughout. And so would the majority of players. How can you expect me, they would argue, to make a free bid on a four card suit at the four level? The funny part of it is that if I had been dealer on the hand and opened one Diamond, all these people would have supported me without hesitation. And when I subsequently bid Hearts, they would have looked on their Heart holding with approval and cooperated in any slam try I might make. Yet when, by bidding three Clubs, I bid *both* of these suits at the same time—for that is what it amounts to—they remain silent. Because I have not, in actual words, bid the suits themselves, they are seized with panic.

"How can I bid a four card suit at the four level! ! ! "

"You're not, blast you! You are supporting me. The only difference is that you are going to play the hand."

When I passed the bid of five Clubs, it was not because I was unaware that partner belonged to the great majority. I feared it, but I was even more afraid that he might hold a totally unsuitable hand. And, if he did, my intermediates were far too weak to prevent a debacle. Mine is the sort of hand that, on a misfit, can go down a fortune. In fact, in my opinion, I had already overbid it when I bid three Clubs. I simply dared not take the gamble of bidding again. Cowardly possibly, but there it is.

Now there may be some of you who would have bid over four Clubs on the East hand, but would you have bid over four Clubs if your hand had been the following?

♠ : x x x
♡ : x x x
◊ : K x x x
♣ : x x x

The point is that you should. Emphatically, you should. Your K, x, x, x is beyond price. Partner has asked you to bid one of the red suits and you have the good luck to hold four cards headed by an honor in one of them. You must let him know about it. Even if your diamonds are a shade worse—say J, x, x, x —it is debatable whether you should make a free bid or not. Personally, I think you should.

Let me offer a simple suggestion for estimating the value of these small hands. Do not worry about trying to visualize your partner's holding. It's very hard work, and half the time you won't be right anyway.

There is a much simpler way.

Look at your hand and decide how much *worse* it might be. Partner's bids or bid will always indicate what suits he is interested in. The rest follows automatically.

Take the following quite common situation. You hold:

♠ : Q x x x x
♡ : K x
♢ : x x x
♣ : x x x

Your are vulnerable and your opponents are not. The opponent on your left deals and bids one Diamond. Your partner doubles. Next hand passes. You bid one Spade. The opener bids three Diamonds. Your partner four Spades. Next hand five Diamonds. What do you do?

Now if you gaze at your own miserable collection and wonder what are the chances of getting eleven tricks out of it, you will clearly depress yourself into passing. And if you try to visualize your partner's hand, you will lose yourself in the labyrinths of assortments he might be holding. But reflect instead how much *worse* your hand might be. You have made a forced reponse. So, as far as your partner is concerned, you might be holding four little Spades and a bust. Yet he seemed to think this was enough for you to make four Spades. Now your hand is much better than that. In the first place, you hold a five suiter to an honor. Secondly you hold the Heart King—an invaluable card as your partner is marked with a strong holding in that suit. Clearly you should bid five Spades in your sleep. Because, clearly, you should expect to make it, and the penalty against non-vulnerable opponents cannot be enough to compensate for not bidding it.

Alter your holding a little. Take away the King of Hearts and replace it with the King of Diamonds. Now your five Spade

[64]

bid is doubtful. The King of Diamonds is of no value whatever to your partner.

I have said it is a waste of energy to bother trying to visualize your partner's holding. But here are some of the hands he might have to justify his bidding.

♠ : A K J x ♠ : K J 10 9 ♠ : A K x x x
♡ : A J 10 x x ♡ : A Q J x x ♡ : Q J 10 9 8
◇ : x ◇ : x ◇ : x
♣ : K Q J ♣ : A Q J ♣ : A Q

and so on. Elementary, isn't it.

Finally, as the supreme example of bidding bad hands, let me resurrect a hand from my once notorious article "Master Bids" published in the *British Bridge World* in 1936. This article, which was entirely devoted to examples of bidding up bad hands, excited a great many jeers at the time and some of the "master bids" I suggested were brushed aside as "too fantastic for discussion." But this particular bid, at first sight the most fantastic of all, was reluctantly admitted to be correct.

Briefly, it was suggested that you should bid a grand slam holding one King and a complete Yarborough. This was the hand:

♠ : x x x
♡ : K x
◇ : x x x x
♣ : x x x x

You were East and the bidding went as follows:

NORTH	EAST	SOUTH	WEST
1 ◇	Pass	2 ♣	2 ◇
3 ♣	Pass	3 ◇	4 ♣!
4 ◇	Pass	5 ♣	5 ◇!!
Pass	5 ♠!	Pass	6 ♠!!!!
Pass	?		

I suggested that a bid of seven Spades from you now stands out a mile.

What it boiled down to was this. Partner, by sheer bullying, has pulled you out of a tepid preference for spades rather than Hearts. On the strength of this tepid preference, he has bid six Spades. And you have the King of Hearts—the King of the other suit he is interested in. There is no reason why you should hold that King. Nothing in your bidding has suggested that

[65]

you can conceivably be holding it. Therefore, he is quite prepared for you to make six Spades without it. Therefore, equally clearly, you can make seven Spades with it.

If you insist, you can start constructing partner's possible holding. There aren't so many this time. He must hold either thirteen cards in the two majors or twelve cards in the majors and one of the outside Aces. Or . . .

But no matter what hand you construct for him, as long as it justifies his bidding, seven Spades must be on ice.

Now I admit that, in practice, you would be unlikely to make the master bid of "seven" on your holding. For one thing, you would need complete confidence in your partner. Still, it does show what I mean about bidding up bad hands.

(e) COMPETITIVE BIDDING

The cards are freak. Both sides are bidding freely. The bidding soars to dizzy heights. Presently the critical point is reached. You have to make a decision. Are you going to double them or are you going to bid one more? Thousands of points may hang on your judgment.

Now, I cannot teach you judgment, but I can suggest a very simple method by which the thousands you may gain by your decision still remain, while the thousands you might lose dwindle into hundreds.

It is this: *When in doubt, bid one more.*

The argument is purely mathematical and unanswerable. You have bid up to four Spades and the enemy have overbid with five Hearts. Both sides are vulnerable. You do not think they can make five Hearts but they might. You do not think you can make five Spades, but again, you might, and you are pretty certain you won't be more than one down.

Let us look at the mathematics of it. Consider your maximum loss first. You bid five Spades, are doubled and, horror, go down two. Greater horror still, you find the enemy would have been down two doubled in five Hearts. This is, of course, an extreme case and suggests that perhaps the decision is not so close as you thought it was. But even at that, your loss is one thousand points.

Take a more normal result of your wrong view. You bid five Spades, go down one doubled, and find you could have defeated five Hearts by one trick. Your cost is 400 points.

And now take the other extreme. You double five Hearts and they make it. They score 300 plus 500 for game plus 50 for doubled contract = 850. And now you find that you could have

[66]

made five Spades and scored 850 yourself. Your wrong view has now cost you 1700 points.

And if your competitive bidding has taken you into the slam zone, you have to be even more careful. Anything can happen on these freak hands, and personally, when it comes to slams, I am quite prepared to be a thousand points out on my decision to bid one more (500 points either way) than take the chance of the enemy making a slam when I might be making one myself.

In the Gold Cup Final, Lederer versus Ingram, the Lederer team was unwilling to take that chance. It cost them over 2000 points. Ingram won the match of 100 boards by 2300 points. The hand in question is the most perfect illustration of the argument in favor of bidding one more—in case. And it happened in practice.

Here it is together with Lederer's analysis, as it appeared in the *Sunday Referee* and reprinted in the *British Bridge World.*

Most Discussed Hand of the Year. Mr. Lederer's Analysis

"What is likely to be the most discussed hand of the year occurred last month in the Gold Cup final between Messrs. Ingram and Lederer. Ingram won an exciting match by some 2300 points, thus adding the Gold Cup to his well-earned Southport Bowl. Our heartiest congratulations. Almost the whole of his winning lead was established on this one deal:

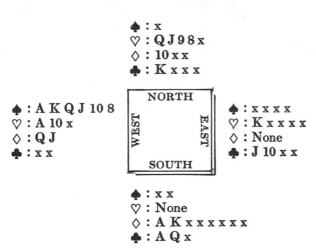

North—South vulnerable. West deals.

[67]

Here is the bidding of the hand:

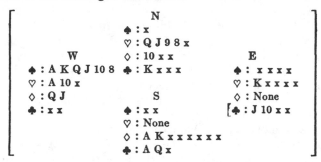

		N		
		♠ : x		
		♡ : Q J 9 8 x		
	W	◊ : 10 x x		E
♠ : A K Q J 10 8	♠ : K x x x		♠ : x x x x	
♡ : A 10 x			♡ : K x x x x	
◊ : Q J		S		◊ : None
♣ : x x	♠ : x x		[♣ : J 10 x x	
		♡ : None		
		◊ : A K x x x x x		
		♣ : A Q x		

Room 1

WEST	NORTH	EAST	SOUTH
Hughes	Lederer	Ingram	Rose
4 ♠	Pass	Pass	5 ◊
Pass	Pass	5 ♠	Pass
Pass	Double		

Diamond 10 led. West made 11 tricks.* 750 to Ingram.

Room 2

WEST	NORTH	EAST	SOUTH
Dodds	Simmons	Kosky	Newmark
2 ♠	Pass	3♣	4◊
4 ♠	5 ◊	Pass	Pass
Double	Pass	5 ♠	6 ◊
Pass	Pass	Double	

Heart Ace led. South made 12 tricks. 1490 to Ingram.
Net Result; 2240 to Ingram.

And here is Mr. Lederer's analysis, as it appears in the *Sunday Referee*:

"Now for my comments. The first impression is that it is difficult to attach the blame for the disaster to any particular bid or player, for all the decisions are extremely close.

"In Room 1 Mr. Hughes's opening bid of four Spades has rushed the bidding to such an extent that not one of the players

---

*North is squeezed in Clubs and Hearts.

knows anything about the hand. On his freak hand, Mr. Rose cannot tell whether opponents can make five Spades or whether he can get six Diamonds. Rather than make a decision, he says 'no bid' to five Spades and passes me the buck.

"I know even less about the hand than my partner, so the best I can do is to pass the buck by doubling, which shows that my hand does contain some value. Mr. Rose now passed.

"Had the contest been decided on match points his final pass could not be criticized. But as the match was played on aggregate scores, he should have bid six Diamonds.

"Here are my reasons:

"(a) On his hand six Diamonds, in view of my double, is quite probable, and in any event is unlikely to be defeated by more than one trick.

"(b) Five Spades, on the bidding, cannot be set more than two tricks at the outside and might even be made.

"(c) If he bids six Diamonds, is doubled, goes one down and finds that five Spades could have been set two tricks, he has chucked 500 points, which is not fatal.

"(d) By passing, he is risking about 2000 points. He is laying 4-1 that his pass is correct. The hand does not warrant these odds.

"Much the same argument applies to Room 2, but even more forcibly, as the bidding there had made the danger of a successful six Diamond contract very apparent.

"Mr. Kosky, by first passing five Diamonds and then rescuing the double into five Spades, had made it quite clear that his hand was worthless defensively. That Mr. Dodds realized the danger is shown by his pass of six Diamonds after having doubled five Diamonds. His pass is good Bridge (a double of six Diamonds would have been shocking) but it is not good enough. He had made a two bid without, under my system, the qualifications for it, and his partner has now announced a defenseless hand.

"Obviously, on simple arithmetic, he cannot take the chance of letting opponents play the hand in six Diamonds, even if it should turn out that they cannot make it. He cannot be many down in six Spades and he has his honors to compensate. His hand is much too bad even to pass the decision to his partner.

"By passing, he says: 'Now that I know you've got a bust, I cannot double six Diamonds. But I am still too strong defensively to sacrifice with six Spades. If you've got anything at all they cannot make their contract.'

"And his hand is not good enough for such a message. Kosky,

who does hold a King and a Jack and has heard his partner open with a two bid, cannot be criticized for doubling."

Personally, I do not agree with Mr. Lederer's double. I think he would have been wiser to have bid six diamonds. After all his partner has found a bid at the five level vulnerable. It cannot cost much.

But again, Willie Rose should never have put his partner in that position. Once he has *not* been doubled in five Diamonds by either opponent (a big consideration, this) he should have bid six Diamonds himself. In fact, at this stage, he would have been risking far less in bidding six himself than he had already risked when he bid five.

Otherwise I have no other comments on the analysis.

CHAPTER FIVE

The Points You Lose
NOT Doubling

THIS CHAPTER is loaded with dynamite.

Earlier in the book I bawled you out for doubling slams with holdings on which a double to you seemed automatic. Now I am going to urge you to double a different type of contract on holdings that appear to be inadequate—hence the dynamite. For it is well known that nothing annoys a partner as much as an unsuccessful double; while doubling opponents into game is almost beyond the pale.

So, if you are nervous, stop reading now—or you may get fascinated.

The theory of doubling is the least understood theory in Contract Bridge. A mass of research has been poured into every other phase of the game with a large lake of resultant literature into which the student may dip. But doubling has been ignored. Certain sidelights of it, informatory doubles, lead directing doubles, have received their share of attention, but the basic principles of doubling—ordinary straightforward honest-to-goodness business doubling—have been taken for granted. In the whole literature of Bridge I know of no single book that has made a serious attempt to analyze the theory of doubling, and that gives the reader at least some hint as to when to double, when not to double, when to leave a double in, and when to take it out.

Even the very elementals, the mere mathematics of doubling, are seldom stressed. The Bridge player is left to find them out for himself. And how well he does it can be seen by the number of players who still double a small slam holding two Aces. Not by you, by now, of course!

How, then, can they be expected to measure a double in anything except the number of Aces and Kings and trumps they may be holding? It is not fair to expect a Bridge player, spoon-fed from his first deal in every other department of the game by every player who considers himself superior, to work it out for himself. And how can he possibly get it right?

Let me try and do a spot of spoon-feeding.

I have only a chapter to devote to the subject. And since starting to marshal my data I have become aware that I should like a book. Perhaps later I may have the opportunity to write such a book. But all I can attempt here is a short analysis of basic principles which I hope may set you thinking along the right lines.

Let us first of all consider the varying conditions under which business doubles occur. At first sight there appear to be a great many, but, ignoring all the minor variations, they boil down to two main situations.

(1) When your opponents have monopolized the bidding.

(2) When they have not.

These are the two basic situations, fundamentally different, and calling for quite a different technique for their successful exploitation. The essential difference is this:—

In the first case your double is final. Partner has not bid and is not being consulted. You double because you think you can defeat the contract and that will be the best result on the hand. The responsibility is all yours. It is, in its essence, a solo flight.

In the second case the responsibility can be shared. Your partner has bid. There is a possible contract of your own in the offing; and your double now becomes an expression of opinion that this will give you the best result on the hand. If your partner does not like the double he can take it out. In fact I classify this type of double as "A Proposal to Partner."

Solo Flight. Proposal to partner. Clearly the requirements are very different.

And now let us study the requirements for each.

SOLO FLIGHTS

The first thing to get into your head is that, though the responsibility is all yours, you are not doubling on your hand alone, but on the combined value of the two hands. You can see your own thirteen cards, you have heard the bidding, you can estimate your partner's probable strength. If you still think you can defeat the contract—go ahead and double.

[72]

But remember in your estimate that it is *not* true that:
THE BIGGER THE HAND THE BETTER THE
DOUBLE.
There is such a thing as a hand being too good.
It must have happened to you a score of times. Think back.
How often have you not sat gloating over some such collec-
tion as this:

♠ : A 10 9
♡ : K Q 10
◇ : A K J x x
♣ : K x

and waited patiently while the enemy has bid up to three No
Trump. Rubbing your hands you have doubled. And then the
unbelievable happens.

The enemy makes three No Trump. Or four No Trump. And
sometimes they even have the cheek to re-double.

Think back. How often has it happened? How often have
you sat there impotently while the declarer has waltzed his way
to his contract, forcing you to lead away from your tenaces,
putting you to embarrassing discards and squeezing you for an
overtrick as a final insult. How often has it happened?

And it is not bad luck. It will happen most of the time when
your hand is as strong as this. Because it is much too strong.
It is in fact so strong that it is quite clear that the enemy are
overbidding and must have a long suit somewhere to compensate
for it. And it is also quite clear that if they can establish and
run that suit before you can establish your diamonds you will
be put to a series of impossible discards, and they are going to
get away with their overbidding because all the strength against
them is concentrated in one hand.

For, unless your opponents are complete lunatics, your partner
has one of the nicest Yarboroughs ever dealt to anyone.

And if you still think your hand is strong enough to defeat
three No Trump with a Yarborough in your partner's hand, well,
let us play out such a hand and see what happens.

You are sitting West, holding the hand in question, when
North, the dealer, bids one Club. East passes mournfully, South
bids two No Trump. You pass waiting. North bids three No
Trump confidently. East and South pass. You double. North
looks less confident, wriggles a bit, but finally passes. All pass.

You lead the King of Diamonds and dummy goes down.

This is the situation as you see it.

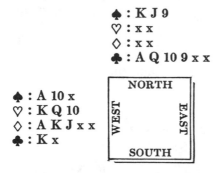

♠ : K J 9
♡ : x x
◊ : x x
♣ : A Q 10 9 x x

♠ : A 10 x
♡ : K Q 10
◊ : A K J x x
♣ : K x

A filthy opening bid, followed by a gambling three No Trump, bid confidently to frighten off doublers. But you were too strong to be frightened. Still you concede North full credit for sticking with the double. Clearly he is hoping for six tricks in Clubs and the other three from Heaven.

Come to think of it South has not got so much either. The only high cards missing are the Queen of Spades, the Ace, Jack of Hearts, the Queen of Diamonds and the Jack of Clubs. Clearly he holds them all. And equally clearly you are not going to defeat this contract.

Try it any way you like, with any opening lead you like. Even assuming the Diamonds are stopped only once, the contract is cold. By the time the declarer has run his Clubs you are in trouble with your discards and can be squeezed or end played according to your choice.

Note that I have been very fair in the example I have chosen. I have made opponents as near lunatics as possible. I have not even given North a seven card Club suit. Actually, against your holding, a seven card suit is more probable than not. And in that case you must take four tricks quickly or you will be squeezed into allowing declarer to make four No Trump.

I do not go as far as to advise you never to double three No Trump on this type of hand. Only don't expect to set them too many; and don't be too surprised if they make it.

You hand is much to good.

But now suppose we make your hand weaker, and remove from it the Ace of Spades and the King of Clubs, and give only one of these cards to your partner. The King of Clubs for preference. This leaves your hand as follows:

[74]

♠ : 10 x x
♡ : K Q 10
♢ : A K J x x
♣ : x x

Now the opponents are no longer near lunatics. With the Ace of Spades in their hands the bidding is quite sound, and if you double it is clearly a gambling double. And yet the contract, on the hand as I have now given it, will be defeated a comfortable two tricks. For you open with the King of Diamonds, switch to the King of Hearts, and now merely wait for your partner to get in with the King of Clubs and lead another Diamond.

Interesting—isn't it? Your own hand is weaker, the opponents are a whole Ace stronger, and yet the contract is defeated.

And this brings us to a point which every Bridge player knows perfectly well through painful experience, both in defending a hand and in playing the dummy, but which very few seem to remember while the bidding is in progress.

It is not your combined strength that counts, so much as the way that strength is divided between the two hands.

(a) ♠ : A 10 x
  ♡ : K Q 10
  ♢ : A K J x x
  ♣ : K x

(b) ♠ : 10 x x
  ♡ : K Q 10
  ♢ : A K J x x
  ♣ : x x

If, with the Clubs bid over me, I *must* double three No Trump on one of these hands, I would far rather double on Hand (b). For there, at least, there is a chance that partner holds the Club suit and can lead through a Diamond—while in Hand (a) I know that the Clubs will be run off against me.

In hand (a) I hold such strength that opponents must be overbidding and partner is marked with a Yarborough. In hand (b) partner cannot hold very much, but he can hold something. And that may make all the difference.

You are not doubling on your own hand alone, but on the combined value of the two hands. In the first case I have quoted, your partner is marked with a Yarborough or near Yarborough. In the other case he is marked with quite a good hand and action may be taken accordingly.

In every contract reached by your opponents there is some sort of inference as to the strength held by your partner. If the opponents stop at four Spades, and you hold a Yarborough—there is an inference that your partner must hold a few high cards or they must have a slam. If one opponent refuses every opportunity to support the other in a suit in which you your-

[75]

self hold only a singleton there is not only a clear inference that he dislikes that suit, but that your partner has the rest of it. If opponents stop at two No Trump and you have only four points in high cards, it is clear that your partner must hold between 12 and 14. And so on.

And the better the opponents the more certain your inferences. And the weaker they are the less certain you can be. And against complete duds you cannot infer anything at all. For as they don't know what they are doing themselves, how can you possibly deduce anything from what they are doing?

So, for the purposes of this chapter, you are playing against reasonably good opponents.

Now, the moment you stop looking at your hand alone and start inferring strength from the opponents bidding you will realize that there are two ways in which a final contract is reached.

(a) Confidently.

(b) Eventually.

The confident contracts are those in which at least one of the opponents has not made a sign off bid during the auction. For instance:

	1.	2.	3.
North:	One Spade	One Spade	One Spade
South:	Two Hearts	Three Spades	Two Diamonds
North:	Four Hearts	Four Spades	Two Spades
South:	——	——	Three No Trump

In the first two examples neither opponent has at any time signed off, and either of them can hold an undisclosed balance of strength. It may not be a very great balance, for neither has made a slam try—but it may be quite enough to re-double. Or of course they may have stretched their hands to the limit and beyond it. In the third example North has signed off with two Spades, but South has jumped to three No Trump. And again he may have enough to spare to re-double; or he may have overbid his hand.

One point about this confident bidding is that there is nothing beyond your hand, to tell you whether the opponents are stretching or bidding with something to spare. As long as either opponent's hand may hold undisclosed strength you cannot infer your partner's holding with anything approaching accuracy. And you cannot double unless you are sure you have them down in your own hand. And pretty sure at that. And unless you are so sure, then the contract is not worth doubling. For confident bidding seldom goes down much; and you are redoubled with an alarming frequency.

[76]

These, then, are the doubles to avoid—the doubles of "confident" contracts on good hands that are not good enough. Yet these are the doubles that are most frequently made, while the players that indulge in them allow masses of "eventual" contracts to escape unscathed and go down in a succession of fifty points each.

And all because they have never reflected that, whereas in a "confident" contract partner's strength can only be hoped for, in an "eventual" contract it is practically guaranteed.

I hope you all know what I mean by an eventual contract. It is a contract just staggered into after both partners have shown the limit of their strength. And it is occurring all the time. For instance, take this typical example:

North:	One Spade
South:	Two Diamonds
North:	Two Spades
South:	Two No Trump
North:	Three No Trump

Over two Diamonds North has bid two Spades, not forcing under any system that I have ever heard of, and showing a clearly limited hand. Over two Spades South has bid two No Trump, showing a fair hand (else he would have passed) but denying the strength to bid three No Trump. North has managed to find the extra strength to bid one more for game—but clearly neither side has anything to spare.

Now I do not say that this contract is seldom made; it is made quite often. But it goes down nearly as often and not infrequently it goes down quite a lot.

The result depends on how the opposing cards lie for a declarer. When they lie well, he makes his contract. When they lie badly, he goes down. When they lie very badly, he goes down a lot.

But when they lie very badly, the opposing strength is divided between the two hands, so for the moment, he is going down a lot *undoubled*, while the defenders are looking at one another, shaking their heads, and agreeing that neither of them had a double.

And that is nonsense. What they mean is that neither of them knew enough to diagnose that *together* they had a double. For, as neither of them had bid, neither felt entitled to place the other with any strength at all. And that is just bad thinking— a relic of early teaching that "a bid shows strength and a pass shows weakness." It is true most of the time. But not all of the time.

[77]

Once you get it into your head that a pass does not compel you to assume that your partner has a Yarborough until proved otherwise, it is an easy transition to arrive at the point where you can recognize the occasions when your partner is definitely marked with some strength on the bidding. And once you can recognize these occasions, the diagnosis of the double becomes very simple.

All you have to do is to look at your own hand and decide whether the cards in it are lying well or badly for the defense.

Sometimes you will be unable to form an opinion. Sometimes it will be clear that they could not lie worse. But sometimes it will seem to you that they could not be lying better.

And then you will know that you have a double.

To return to the bidding I have given earlier:

North:	One Spade
South:	Two Diamonds
North:	Two Spades
South:	Two No Trump
North:	Three No Trump

Suppose that against this bidding you are holding the following hand:

♠ : K J 9 x   ♡ : Q x x   ◊ : x   ♣ : Q J 10 9 x

Now, if you are sitting West, this is not so good. You are sitting under the Spades and your partner is sitting under the Diamonds. The indications are that the cards are lying well for the declarer. True, the contract might still be defeated—for the cards might not be lying so well for him as the bidding indicates. For instance, if South holds the Queen of Spades your prospects are much improved—but the odds are against the double. You won't be re-doubled, but you won't set him many tricks and he might even make an overtrick.

But, if you are sitting East, this is a peach of a hand. You are sitting over the Spades, and whatever Diamond honors your partner may hold are sitting over the bidder. And in addition you have a suit which can be established in two rounds—or on one round if your partner has an honor in Clubs. And why shouldn't he have? The bidding has marked him with quite a lot of high cards.

The double stands out. It might be worth as much as four down. And even if the cards do not turn out to lie as badly for the declarer as you thought, the chances are that he will still go down. And he will certainly not make an overtrick. The odds are all in your favor.

[78]

Take another example of everyday bidding:

North:	One Spade
South:	Two Spades
North:	Three Spades
South:	Four Spades

You hold: ♠ : A K x   ♥ : A x x   ♦ : x x x x   ♣ : x x x

There is not even the ghost of a reason for doubling. There is no reason at all why your partner should be able to produce a trick. He possibly holds a few high cards in a side suit; but high cards in side suits are uncertain values against a suit contract.

The opponents have reached four Spades missing the two top honors in the suit. They will have their compensating values elsewhere. Your hand does not contain anything in the nature of a surprise for them. The declarer will have allowed for losing tricks in trumps.

But, supposing you hold:

♠ : Q J 10 9
♥ : x x x
♦ : x x x
♣ : x x x

Now, that is quite different. Declarer still has high card strength against him—only now your partner holds it. The bidding shows that. But he is not reckoning to lose many tricks in trumps—one at the outside. And you have quite a nasty surprise for him. Your partner's hand may well be something like:

♠ : None
♥ : K Q x x
♦ : A J x x
♣ : x x x x x

or even better.

If your partner is educated in diagnosis he might well double four Spades himself. The fact that he is void in trumps is an incentive. It means that you must have quite a few.

There is a great deal to be achieved in the intelligent doubling of suit contracts by inferring your partner's trump holding. A secondary suit is usually bid on a four card suit. The support is seldom more than four cards. If, therefore, you hold a singleton in that suit, your partner is marked with four. And if you have a void, he may have five. It helps quite a lot if you realize it.

And so my advice on solo flight doubles boils down to this:

[79]

Against confident bidding, wait for a moral certainty. But against eventual contracts, when you can infer that the cards are badly placed for the declarer, double on a couple of picture cards and hope.

Of course, inevitably there will be cases where you will have inferred incorrectly. And then you must resign yourself to accepting the reproaches of your partner who will want to know how you dared double when he held two honor tricks and they still made it. Apologize, and pass on to the next hand. On no account explain that on the bidding you expected him to hold three honor tricks and that he has let you down by only holding two. He won't understand.

And, in any case, you do not wish him to learn, and start diagnosing doubles when you are the declarer!

But quite seriously, reflect on all the contracts that you have defeated several tricks because "neither of you had a double." I think you will find that it is worth being wrong sometimes.

PROPOSAL TO PARTNER

It is well known that the juiciest penalties are obtained by doubling opponents at low contracts. Modern bidding has improved enough to make really satisfying doubles of high contracts, voluntarily reached, a rarity; and, as we have seen, the ones that can be successfully doubled are defeated more on the rocks of distribution than on any unsoundness in the bidding. Occasionally a plum from a super-misfit and taking-each-other-out-partners may fall into your lap; but that is of financial interest only. You did not even have to pick it.

It is at the low levels, where players are tempted to butt in with a bid, that the opportunities still occur. And most of them are still allowed to escape. For, unless the player sitting over the butter-in was about to bid the suit himself, he seldom doubles. Either because he does not know how, or because, as happens frequently in my own case, I cannot trust my partner-of-the-moment to take out the double if he does not like it.

And therefore I offer you this suggestion.

Arrange with as many of your partners as you can to treat all business doubles at the one or two level as purely tentative. Take the following bidding:

NORTH	EAST	SOUTH	WEST
1 ♠	2 ◊	Double	Pass

The majority of Norths wouldn't dream of disturbing this double unless they had opened under strength, or with a psychic, or because they would rather try for game "with a hundred honors, partner"! But on all other occasions they will pass, satisfied that so long as they have their two plus honor tricks, nothing else is open to them. And while this situation exists, it is clearly impossible to make speculative doubles. For your opponents will make far too many of these contracts with overtricks, and your partner will be demanding indignantly what the devil you doubled on.

Clearly with this bidding it is ridiculous to double two Diamonds on such a holding as:

♠ : x
♡ : K x x x
◇ : J 9 x
♣ : A Q x x x

And yet, to my mind, this is not only the best bid on the hand; it is the only possible bid. Study the alternatives.

Two Hearts? Clearly misleading—the suit is too weak.

Three Clubs? Now, what do you expect your partner to bid over that? Three No Trump? Is there any reason to think he can make it? Or Three Hearts? Now, that really is obliging of him.

Actually you know as well as I do that over three Clubs he is far more likely to rebid his Spades at the three level.

And, what are you going to bid then?

But a double of two Diamonds in this instance has endless potentialities; and, if partner's hand really fits, it might turn out to be sensational. Suppose your partner holds:

(a) ♠ : A K x x x
♡ : A x x x
◇ : Q x x
♣ : x

The contract can hardly fail to be defeated at least two tricks —probably three, and possibly four. And yet there is no game in the hand for your side.

But how can you reach for this dazzling prospect if your partner is liable to pass your double on some such hand as:

(b) ♠ : A K x x x
♡ : Q J x x x
◇ : None
♣ : K x x

Here you have a probable small slam in Hearts and the enemy will certainly make two Diamonds, if not three.

[81]

So what are you to do if your partner stoically regards your doubles as entirely your own business, considering his responsibility at an end as long as he has his bid? If you don't double, you may be missing a sizable penalty with no good contract of your own. If you do double, they may make it with an overtrick and there might be a small slam of your own in the hand.

Clearly, your partner must learn to co-operate. He must be taught that your double of low contracts is not an order to pass, but merely a suggestion to be considered. And when he has grasped that, he must be taught what the features are in his hand that should cause him either to accept or refuse the invitation. And before you can teach him that, you must understand yourself what the features are in your own hand that cause you to favor a double rather than finding a contract of your own.

Let us therefore get down to study the qualifications that make a good tentative business double of an intervening bid.

The essential point to grasp is that a double is not a success unless it scores more points than you would have scored in your own contract. For instance, if you double one Spade and set it seven tricks, not vulnerable (1300), it is not a success, but a downright failure, if *you* can make seven No Trump, vulnerable.

Therefore, the first essential to bear in mind, when making a tentative business double, is that it should, at the moment that it is made, seem to you your best prospect of collecting the maximum number of points on the deal. And that is the message your double sends to your partner. Later on, you may change your mind—but that is later on.

Thus, if it seems probable to you, after your partner's opening bid, that the hand contains a game, then clearly the points you expect to gain from the double must exceed the value of the game. As a rough guide this means that you have to defeat a vulnerable overbid by three tricks and a non-vulnerable overbid by four tricks to show any worth-while profit. And that (except against the rapturous "it was only an intervening bid, partner" butter-in—now rapidly becoming extinct) is a lot to ask, particularly if your hands fit. And the very fact that you can see prospects of a game argues that you have a fit in the suit bid by your partner.

It has probably never occurred to you that a fit in your partner's suit is a *disadvantage* in doubling a contract in another suit. Reflect on it and it becomes obvious. The fact that, between you, you hold most of a suit, means that the enemy holds few of it. And therefore you cannot hope to make many tricks

[82]

in that suit. If your partner bids one Heart and you hold five Hearts, you are unlikely to make more than one trick in the suit and you might well make none. And you have an excellent prospect of game in Hearts. But if you hold a singleton Heart, you will almost certainly make all the high Hearts your partner holds, and ruff some of the small ones in the bargain. And your prospects of a game in Hearts are poor.

Therefore, as a general rule, a tentative double should not contain too good a fit in your partner's suit. Three cards should be the extreme limit. With four the result is unlikely to be good. And with five the loss, except in very rare cases, is a certainty.

To my mind the ideal tentative double contains a singleton in partner's suit, no particularly good suit of your own, a few trumps to an honor, and a total point count of about nine. A hand like the one that just doubled two Diamonds—a hand on which prospects of game seem remote and where as little as two down doubled is an excellent result.

This, then, is the tentative double. But what are the features in your partner's hand that should decide whether he should leave the double in or take it out?

Well—there is only one governing feature that is decisive. That is his trump-holding. All the other considerations are subsidiary to it.

And the rule is this: The better the trump-holding, the less strength is needed elsewhere to let the double stand. And *vice versa.*

Here are the rules I have made for myself for low level doubles. With three trumps or more, leave the double in even on the weakest of opening bids.

With a doubleton in trumps, leave the double in on any good opening bid of three honor tricks or more. With a singleton take out the double on anything under $3\frac{1}{2}$ to four honor tricks. With a void—take it out regardless of anything.

For it is *not* an advantage to be void in the suit your partner has doubled at a low level. It means not only that your partner must have a lot, but also that dummy will have quite a few.

And if dummy has quite a few trumps, a double of a low contract is not going to be a success. But you know that as well as I do. You have seen far too many powerful trump holdings ruined by dummy's possession of something like 9, 8, 6 to dispute the point. If your partner could only have led trumps through even once—it would have made all the difference. But your partner couldn't. He was void.

Now, a few pages back, when we were discussing a double of

[83]

an enemy contract at a high level, I wrote that a void in the enemy's suit was an incentive, for it meant that your partner might have quite a few. Now, here, for a low level double, I am insisting that a void should deter you.

But it is not a contradiction. It is a logical extension.

In a high level double you do not expect to make more tricks than the declarer. Success in a high level double relies on high-card tricks plus whatever trump tricks may be outstanding.

Therefore it is far better to hold a void in trumps than three small ones. It increases the chances of your partner's having a trump trick.

But for any worth-while success in a double of a low contract you must take more tricks than the declarer. It is, to all intents and purposes, playing the hand in the declarer's suit. If, for instance, you double two Spades and set it three tricks, it means that you have made eight tricks with Spades as trumps —i.e. that you have made two Spades yourself.

Viewed from this angle everything becomes beautifully clear. It is obvious now why it is necessary to have a few cards in the suit partner has doubled.

For if partner doubles two Spades and you leave it in with a void, it means in effect that you are permitting him to play a Spade contract with a void in his suit.

And, you never do that if you can help it, do you?

Thus, every extra trump you hold is invaluable. Not only does it increase your own joint trump holding, but it decreases the delcarer's holding. If you hold three trumps, dummy is unlikely to hold more than a singleton. With a doubleton you can lead trumps through twice, which may permit your partner to draw trumps.

Even with a singleton, you can lead through once. But you cannot lead through with a void. So, unless your partner's trump holding is so strong that he can afford to draw trumps himself, declarer will make his small trumps (and far too many tricks) for your satisfaction.

For, in low level doubles, it is just as essential for the defense to stop declarer making his small trumps as, in higher contracts, it is essential for the declarer to stop the defense.

There are, of course, hands on which it is better for declarer not to draw trumps but play for a cross ruff. Just so there are such hands for the defense. You can recognize them as you meet them. They in no way effect the principle that most of the time it pays to draw trumps. And that in low level doubles the defense can seldom draw trumps if the doubler's partner is void.

[84]

Your Battlefield

THINK OF a Bridge Club. Any Bridge Club. *Your* Bridge Club. Here is your battlefield. Here, in concentrating groups of four, are the victims whose money you are proposing to win. Unless, of course, you prefer them to take yours.

Now, just in case you are imagining that the wisdom you have imbibed in the first part of this book is sufficient to make you a winner, let me disabuse you at once. Even if you have absorbed it all—which you haven't—it won't.

For Part 1 concentrated entirely on the technical side of your game, and your technical game is only one half of the reason why you lose at Bridge.

The other half is your psychology.

You may win duplicate matches by playing perfect Book Bridge. But you will never win money in a Bridge Club, not, at any rate, in any Bridge Club that I know. In all of them perfect Book Bridge all the time is the most certain way of losing.

And if you don't believe me, just think back to an individual you've all met—the Unlucky Expert. His bidding is perfect, his play flawless. But he never wins. All his partners let him down.

Poor fellow, whenever I sight him I make straight for his table. If I cut him, our combined extra skill gives us an enormous advantage over the two palookas. And if I cut one of the palookas, all I've got to do is wait for the other palooka to let the Unlucky Expert down. He seldom fails me.

For the Unlucky Expert is so good he cannot bring himself to realize how bad other players can be. Either that, or he is determined to punish them for it—even when they are his

[85]

partners. He will not bring his game down to their level—they must lift theirs to his. He is guaranteed to demoralize, to twittering nit-wittedness, any weak player he cuts.

And this makes him just about the best grub there is in the Bridge world.

Let me quote a hand to show the Unlucky Expert at work. It is a classic example of what can happen to perfect Book Bridge at a Bridge Club.

The Unlucky Expert was having an exhausting rubber. Not only had his palooka unwarrantably taken him out of Three No Trump to go down at Four Spades, but on the very next deal he had left him in Three No Trump when Four Spades was on ice. Now at Game All the Expert picked up the following:

♠ : A J x x x
♡ : A Q J x x
◇ : A K x
♣ : None

and heard his partner open the bidding with a "sulky" one Spade.

Now, even a moderately sensible person would have bid Six Spades and left it at that. A greedy player would have bid Seven Spades and hoped for the best. But the Unlucky Expert was neither sensible nor greedy. He was scientific. And he set out scientifically to discover whether the Grand Slam was there.

Actually it was, for the palooka held:

♠ : K Q 10 x x
♡ : K
◇ : Q J x
♣ : K Q 10 x

But this is what happened.

The Expert forced with three Hearts. The palooka bid a prompt three No Trump. The Expert bid four No Trump (conventional). The palooka huddled and bid a timid five Spades. It was apparent, as far off as the next table, that he hated the whole business. But the Expert had no time for such trifles. All he noted was that his partner had made an encouraging response. (The sign off would have been five Hearts.) He now produced a Master bid. He bid six Clubs.

Now this is really quite a pretty bid. Following a conventional bid of four No Trump it is clearly a cue bid, showing first

[86]

round control of Clubs (either the Ace or a void) agreeing on the Spade suit by implication, giving a perfect picture of his hand and asking partner if he holds the necessary missing cards to bid the Grand Slam.

Unfortunately his partner failed to get the message. He passed quickly with a sigh of relief.

My partner, holding Clubs A, J, 10, x, x, x, was also a palooka. But he had just enough sense to pass.

In stony silence the Unlucky Expert went down seven undoubled.

"Partner," demand his puzzled but indignant palooka, "why didn't you support my Spades?"

Now I have no sympathy at all for the Unlucky Expert on this deal. He deserved all he got. He bid the hand beautifully—just as he would have done if he had been playing with me.

And he wasn't.

And that is what I mean when I tell you that technical excellence alone will not win you any money at a Bridge Club. You must learn to play your players. And your partners more than your opponents. You must learn their strengths, weaknesses, predilections and obstinacies—and allow for them. You will not be able to stop them "fixing" you all the time, but you'll stop them some of the time.

In this part of the book I propose to tell you how to set about it.

It is true that I do not know the particular individuals in your Bridge Club. But I know them well enough for your purpose. For all Bridge Clubs, from the Portland to the tenth-of-a-cent Suburban, are only reproductions of each other in varying degrees of wealth, with the identical assortment of inhabitants. The accents may vary but, from the Bridge point of view, representatives of the various breeds are found in all of them.

If you have never played Bridge in a club, you are probably under the impression that anyone who does is, *ipso facto*, a good player; and you hesitate to enter that charmed circle for fear of finding yourself outclassed. There is no need to hesitate on that score. However bad you may be, there is bound to be somebody in every club who is worse. It is not your own lack of skill that makes a Bridge Club dangerous to your pocket—it is the lack of skill of the other members. Unless you can adapt yourself to it, you're sunk.

Take a look round the room. What a collection!

How are you to adapt yourself to this conglomeration of over-bidders, under-bidders. natural bidders, scientific bidders,

[87]

psychic bidders, dud dummy players, dud defenders, timid old ladies, deaf old men, quarrelers who play Bridge for pleasure, trancers who play to agonize you, and masochists who play to agonize themselves? And the professionals—who will win your money, anyway?

Well, you can forget about the professionals. It is their business to adapt themselves to you and they do it pretty well. In fact, I suggest that you take a few rubbers off one afternoon and sit behind one of them. You will then see him practicing what I am about to preach.

CHAPTER

SEVEN

Don't Teach Your Partner

It is agreed, of course, that you are better than the majority of the players at your club. It is also agreed that they refuse to admit this.

Now, though a teacher may occasionally learn from his pupils, the teacher never likes it. And as most of your pupils fancy themselves fit to be your teachers they won't take kindly to your instructions.

Therefore don't instruct them.

Learn their game. Don't attempt to improve it.

For your own small circle of pet partners, this does not apply. Here the more you get together to discuss, argue and swear at each other the better. But for the great majority—no. Emphatically—no.

In the first place most of them don't want to learn. Secondly, those that do cannot possibly absorb instructions crammed into post-mortems between deals. It can only confuse them.

And there is no one more difficult to play with than a willing, but confused, partner.

The point is that most Bridge players are firmly set in their erring ways. Whatever form of atrocity they favor, they are consistent in it and, once you are aware what the atrocity is, you can take your counter-measures. But try and cure them of their atrocity, and part of the time they will remember, and part of the time they will forget, and the rest of the time they will compromise with half an atrocity and you will never know where you are.

Take a simple example: the man who will bid No Trump with a singleton in your suit. Leave him alone and, at least, you know that when he takes you into No Trump the chances are he has a singleton in your suit. You can act accordingly. But if you exact from him a promise not to do it without "something" in your suit, you will set up such a conflict in his mind between his promise and his natural tendencies that the result will become unpredictable, and you will be guessing every time.

So don't teach your partners. Presently they will be your opponents. And after that they will be cutting into another table altogether.

You never see the professionals offering gratuitous instructions. Sometimes under the relentless pressure of "Did I play it right, partner?" they may be provoked into a denial. But in the main their comments are confined to the occasional "Well done, partner," or the more frequent "Hard luck, partner." They are not there to teach. They are there to win.

It is, perhaps, time that I made it clear what I mean by the term "Bridge professional." Strictly speaking, I suppose, it applies only to the fellow who makes his living playing cards, and admits it, with varying accuracy, on his Income Tax return. In practice, it is promptly hung round the neck of any player known to be playing for higher stakes than he could afford if he were a losing player. Sometimes it is even hung round the neck of such a one who *is* a losing player. I know several of these alleged professionals who invariably end up by knocking some club or other for the simple reason that they are not good enough to be winning players in the school in which they are performing.

From my own point of view, and for the purpose of this book, the definition of a Bridge professional is very simple. It is any player who wins consistently without cheating to do it. I do not care if it is his only source of livelihood, or if he is a captain of industry in his spare time. If he is a constant comfortable winner, year in year out, he is a professional. From that point of view, the late Willie Rose, who was one of the best rubber Bridge players I knew, and a millionaire in the bargain, was a professional. And that well-known professional, Mr. ———, well, no matter—isn't.

And now I'll wait patiently while you tell me that you play Bridge for pleasure and don't care whether you win or lose as long as you enjoy the game.

But I have yet to meet the "I play for pleasure" announcer who gets up after a losing session looking in the least pleased.

Let us be quite cold-blooded about this.

We all play Bridge to win.

Even the wealthy old ladies at the more exclusive clubs,

who contribute their regular $10,000 a year to the professionals, and who are resigned to contributing it and almost budget for it, play to win. They don't expect to, but they hope they will. Try one of them with an offer of taking over their liabilities for a year for $5,000 cash. It would save them $5,000 a year and they could still have all their pleasure of playing. What sort of an answer do you think you'll get?

So let us, at any rate in this book, be frank with each other. After all, you don't have to admit to anyone else that you agree with me.

You may play Bridge for pleasure. You may deliberately have cut yourself into the strongest school you can find because you enjoy a good game. You may be quite prepared to lose and go on losing.

But you would rather win.

Right. Now we can get on.

CHAPTER

EIGHT

Half a Loaf

WHEN YOU first sit down behind your selected professional you will be astonished at the number of bad bids he keeps on making. There is a cold game in the hand. He stops at a part score. He ought to make a Slam try—he doesn't. He has ample to give partner a raise—he can't pass quickly enough. What on earth made you think the fellow was good?

But presently, as you watch, you will notice something else. Most of these bad bids seem to turn out quite nicely. Game was cold but the declarer only made three. A Slam could have been made but the way declarer played the hand he was lucky not to go down at three No Trump. Partner hadn't begun to have his bid.

So presently you start looking at the various partners with whom the bad bids are made, and you realize something else.

The professional is not concerned with playing good Bridge. He is playing practical Bridge. He is not interested in the best theoretical result on a hand—all he cares about is what he can score on it in the actual circumstances. It is no use to him that a small Slam can be made on a squeeze if his partner, who has to play the hand, can't execute a squeeze. Far better to bid and score a game than give the opponents fifty points, and explain to an unbelieving partner later how he could have made the Slam.

In this it will be seen that he is the antithesis of the Unlucky Expert. The Unlucky Expert loses his shirt because he always, irrespective of anything else, tries for the best possible result. The professional tries for the best result possible.

The best result possible. Not the best possible result.

And there you have the principle of successful rubber Bridge —the principle of half-a-loaf or even a quarter-of-a-loaf.

You have got to stop thinking in terms of par on the hand—the best possible result your hands can produce. You must think what is a reasonable result to get on your hand with your present partner. You must limit your ambition to that. And the worse your partner the more limited your ambition.

It is a case of Circumstances Alter Bids.

Thus while it may be right to try for a Grand Slam on a certain hand with one partner, a Small Slam on the same hand would be ample with another, and a mere game, bid and made, quite satisfactory with a third.

And now let us examine in greater detail how this principle of half-a-loaf can be applied in practice to various menaces that lurk in your club and who contribute so largely to your income when they are playing against you. Then, perhaps, they will not take all of it back when they are playing with you.

Meet Mrs. Guggenheim.

But, of course, you have met her already.

Mrs. Guggenheim is Menace Number 1 in every Bridge Club. She is a large, ample woman always on the verge of tears. No one works harder at being good at Bridge. She takes lessons and walks around with a Culbertson summary in her handbag. And she can neither bid nor play a hand. And never will.

Perhaps you are one of the people in your club who refuse to cut into any table containing Mrs. Guggenheim. If this is because she spoils the game, then I won't quarrel with you. But if, as I suspect, it is because you are frightened of cutting her and losing a large rubber, then you are wrong.

In the first place she will cut against you twice for every time she cuts with you. And secondly, if you learn to handle her right, she will lose the majority of her large rubbers against you.

I propose to devote quite a lot of space to the handling of Mrs. Guggenheim. For she is the obvious illustration of the half-loaf theory. Once you have grasped the principles of her treatment, I need only give you the outline for the other menaces and you will have no difficulty in working out the variations for yourself.

The first thing to realize on cutting Mrs. Guggenheim is that you will need twice as many good cards as the opponents to win the rubber. As you are unlikely to get them, it is probable that you will lose the rubber.

Concentrate on making it a small one.

In fact, your tactics on cutting Mrs. Guggenheim must be to get through the rubber as quickly as possible and cut again.

That is where so many players go wrong. They sigh with resignation on cutting her, sigh even more heavily over her mistakes, and yet fight savagely to prolong the rubber.

Remember this. With Mrs. Guggenheim, all sacrifice bidding is out. Normally it is theoretically a good result to go down three hundred points to save the rubber. It is not a good result playing with Mrs. Guggenheim. It is sheer stupidity.

If you sacrifice 300 points to continue a rubber with Mrs. Guggenheim, you are paying to continue fighting under a handicap. You are deliberately prolonging a rubber in which at any moment, in spite of all the care you may lavish on her, your partner may chuck thousands. Three hundred points is too much—the times on which it shows a profit cannot possibly compensate for the further catastrophes it may incur.

You cannot prevent Mrs. Guggenheim deciding to sacrifice "with a hundred honors, partner," but you can at least stop aiding and abetting her.

No. You must decide from the outset that you are losing this rubber as cheaply as possible. If you have the good luck to hold enough cards to win it—remember it is good luck. Don't decide to win the next one.

All this may seem rather rough on Mrs. Guggenheim. If her partners aren't going to contest the rubbers, what chance has she of winning?

The answer is that she has no chance anyway, and that by concentrating on keeping down your losses with her, you are doing her a favor. You are keeping *her* losses down, too.

And, anyway, there is no need to tell Mrs. Guggenheim what you are doing. The poor darling is quite incapable of working it out for herself that you had a cheap four Spade save against that four Heart contract. It will never even occur to her. So don't tell her.

I have had two Mrs. Guggenheims, holding a combined Six Club make, chortling with triumph at defeating a Two Diamond contract, of mine, three tricks, not doubled, not vulnerable. I didn't tell them. Why should I spoil their pleasure?

So do not spoil Mrs. Guggenheim's pleasure. She is certainly paying for it. If you cannot go so far as to show pleasure at cutting her, at least conceal enough of your true emotions to let her feel pleased she has cut you. Try and be one of those people she likes to cut. Sympathize with her mistakes and praise her every time she succeeds in not going down in a cast-iron contract. You will find that she plays twice as well. It will still be appalling, but it will be less appalling.

[94]

As for the actual business of bidding with Mrs. Guggenheim, there is one mistake that everybody (barring, of course, the professional) makes with her, and it is a mistake that you must learn to avoid if you are to attain your limited objective of losing a small rubber.

The mistake of trying to play every hand yourself.

Because the one fault Mrs. Guggenheim does not possess is a desire to play the hand. She knows she cannot play the dummy and is only too glad for you to do it. Her tendency is all to leave you in some impossible contract because "you play them so much better, partner."

So when she does show a strong inclination to play the hand—let her. Even if she makes two tricks less than the hand is worth played in her suit, it will still be probably two tricks more than you can make in yours.

Your bidding of the ordinary hands presents no problem. The hands you are going to play yourself you bid to their full value.

The hands she is going to play you underbid. You don't attempt to play them yourself. You underbid them by one trick, if not more.

For instance, if you have bid One Club on:

♠ : J x x x
♡ : A
◇ : K Q x
♣ : A K J 10 x

and she responds with one Spade, your hand is clearly worth four Spades. Even with a minimum response, there must be a play for game.

But if you bid four Spades and Mrs. Guggenheim has a minimum, there may be a play for game, but it won't be a lay-down, which means that Mrs. Guggenheim almost certainly won't make it.

If you cannot bear the thought of missing a game that is there, even though Mrs. Guggenheim has to play it, go ahead and bid four Spades. Or, if you must play the hand yourself, go ahead and bid three No Trump, and maybe you'll make it.

But, personally, I bid two Spades or, at the outside, three Spades. If Mrs. Guggenheim now bids game, the chances are that the hand will be easy enough for her to tackle. If she passes, I'm quite satisfied. Game may well be there, but not with Mrs. Guggenheim playing the hand. And I would rather score 60 or 90 myself than give the enemy anything from 50 to 500.

Opponents need very little encouragement to double Mrs. Guggenheim.

[95]

And, on the rare occasions that Mrs. Guggenheim passes two Spades and makes four, I apologize, take all the blame, and explain that I did not fancy the hand.

As for the unpredictable and uncontrollable phases of Mrs. Guggenheim's Bridge, there is not much you can do except accept disasters cheerfully when they happen and sympathize with her on her bad luck. This is quite easy to do if you remember (*a*) that the dear old soul did it for the best, and (*b*) will do it twice as often against you.

Mrs. Guggenheim, rabbit though she is, has at least one saving grace. She knows she is a rabbit and is only too glad for you to take control.

This does not apply to the other menaces in the club. They think they are as good as anybody and will strongly resent the idea that you are controlling them.

Therefore, don't let them catch you at it.

This means you will have to make a number of concessions, but it will be worth it for the ensuing harmony.

As any one of these menaces is not noticeably worse than the other, your ambition need no longer be limited to losing a small rubber. You can hope to win it. But the half-loaf theory remains. You must still concentrate on the best practical bid rather than the best theoretical bid.

So do not, however charmingly, point out to your menace where his ideas of the game are wrong. He won't agree. Find out what they are and play them with him.

For instance, take that most common menace—"the man who won't accept a sign-off." However frantically you shriek your weakness at him, he goes on bidding. And the more you sign-off the higher the contract gets.

Say he bids one Club and you respond one Diamond, holding:

♠ : Q x x
♡ : x x
◇ : K 9 x x x x
♣ : x x

and he now bids two No Trump.

With a normal partner your bid is easy. You bid Three Diamonds, which he will pass, and which you expect to make. Or, if he doesn't pass, it means he has the diamonds with you and you can redouble three No Trump.

But with the partner, who can't take a sign-off, a bid of three Diamonds will get a response of three No Trump whether he has the Diamonds or not. Particularly if not. And then three No Trump will be doubled, and go down quite a few.

So you don't bid three Diamonds. You accept his theory that there is no such bid as a sign-off and you pass two No Trump. Let him go down in that undoubled. You haven't got your best result on the hand: but you've got a much better result than if you had bid three Diamonds.

And perhaps, on a later hand, when you hold much the same hand plus an extra Ace, which now gives you ample to bid three No Trump, you can cash in on his blind spot by bidding three Diamonds. He is certain to ignore it and go to three No Trump, and the Unlucky Expert is equally certain to double "on the bidding." Now you can redouble.

And don't let any busybody tell you such tactics are unethical. No good Bridge player can possibly object to them. If it is in order for my opponents to profit from the weaknesses of my partner, why shouldn't I? If they are going to double on the bidding, then I have the right to make the bidding sound the way I please.

Take another type of menace—the elderly ex-Auction Bridge player who will raise your suit on inadequate trump support, perhaps as little as a doubleton honor. It is no use pleading with him not to do it. He is an old man, still living in the old days, when nobody bid a major with less than five of a suit with two honors. And though he will do his best to remember your instructions, he is bound to have lapses.

It is far simpler for you not to bid four-card major suits. And conversely, there is no need to wait for him to rebid a major before supporting it with three small trumps. He will certainly have a five suiter. And this knowledge will be very useful on many hands.

Of course, theoretically, you will miss many "best possible results" by giving up your bidding of four-card majors. But practically, on balance, you will be getting the best results possible.

Passing out of the category of rabbits and on to the bulk of the players more or less your own standard, much the same considerations prevail. But whereas previously your "best results possible" depended mainly on staying within the technical limitations of your rabbit, now—since the skills are more or less equal—you must depend more on that intangible quality known as partnership harmony.

Now it is clearly impossible for you to play in harmony with everybody at the Club. There will be players whose mere presence at your table provokes your worst instincts and your worst Bridge. Admirable citizens probably, but they just rub you the wrong way. There is nothing to be done about this. Exclude them from this argument and, when possible, from your table.

But, for the rest, there is no reason why fair harmony should not be achieved. The essential is a working compromise of each other's fads and fancies, and confidence—or at any rate, an appearance of confidence—in your partner's ability. If you can work up a mutual admiration society for the duration of the rubber, so much the better.

Two admiring mediocre players will always put it all over two quarreling experts.

Now, in order to keep your partner admiring you, you must fall in with his theories of the game, or at least appear to fall in with them. So agree to play any system he prefers with practically any trimmings he may suggest.* If he is an under-bidder, which means he considers himself a sound solid caller ("You can rely on my bids, partner"), let him think he can rely on your bids, too. If he overcalls wildly ("I believe in bidding up my cards"), see that he thinks that you bid them up as well.

This is in essence, the advice given by Ely Culbertson many years ago in his Blue Book. He pointed out that if you overbid with an under-bidder, you would not even matters up but cause him to underbid even more in an effort to counteract your excesses. Whereas if he believed that he could rely on your bidding, he would loosen up himself and better results would be achieved. And *vice versa* for the over-bidder.

Culbertson, however, actually advised you to play your partner's game. I have found, on my own experience, that it is unnecessary to go to quite these lengths. It is quite enough to give the impression that you are playing it.

My own game varies very little whomever I cut or whatever system I have agreed to play. Most of the time I make what seems to me the best bid in the circumstances, whether it is an overbid, an underbid, or even an anti-system bid. And most of the time I get away with it unnoticed.

For, unless some calamity has occurred, few Bridge players take the trouble to work out what you were bidding on. And, so long as your hand doesn't have to go down on the table, you can get away with almost anything.

---

*Asking Bids excepted. Whatever the merits of asking bids, Culbertson himself admits that they are fatal unless properly understood. Not one Bridge player in a thousand understands them properly. Do not, however, make this the reason for refusing to play them with your partner. Plead imperfect comprehension yourself. Turn down his offer to teach you.

Therefore, when I am going to play the hand, I will overbid slightly with my under-bidder, and underbid slightly with my over-bidder, and they will be none the wiser and go on considering me "sound" and "bidder-up" respectively. But if I'm going to be dummy, then the hand that goes down mustn't disappoint them.

For then they might lose confidence.

CHAPTER NINE

They Can't Fool Me!

IT IS well known that the Poker player who is never bluffed is a losing player.

So is the Bridge player who is never psyched.

Just as in Poker, so at Bridge there are moments when the possible cost of calling a bluff is greater than the gain is worth. The good Poker player accepts these situations with a shrug. "So I'm bluffed. So what!"

"So you're psyched. So what!"

It is no part of this book to teach you psychic bidding. If you indulge in it, that must remain your own personal indulgence. And if it is one of the reasons why you lose at Bridge, it is a luxury reason, and this is a book on essentials.

Nobody can compel you to psych.

But you can't stop anybody psyching against you.

That is why I must discuss here the defense against psychics, shut-out bids, and all the other nuisance bids designed to rob you of your rightful heritage. For that is a part of the game in which the majority of players, including the psychic bidders themselves, are amazingly ignorant. Indeed, the ordinary player's only reaction, when he suspects he is being diddled out of something, is to overbid his own hand wildly. It seems to him that because somebody has psyched, his own hand has become twice as good as it really is.

How often have you not heard a player explaining that he would never have bid that Slam normally, only he knew opponents were psyching. How often have you done it yourself?

The majority of the successes achieved by nuisance bids are not in keeping opponents out of makable slams, but in goading them into unmakable ones

Therefore, before we go any further, grasp this point: *Your hand has not improved because opponents may be psyching. It remains exactly as it was. As strong—but no stronger.* You must base your bidding on the values you hold—not on what you think opponents haven't got.

Part of the time your own values will be enough to combat what the enemy is doing. And part of the time they won't and the enemy will win. When you have realized this and cease combatting the inevitable, you will hold these victories to a minimum.

For the secret of satisfactory defense against nuisance bids lies in the paradox that there isn't one.

There is no defense that will work all the time.

The ambition of a nuisance bid is to confuse the opponents, disrupt their communications, put them on the spot, and generally throw a monkey wrench into their bidding machinery. And part of the time the remaining cards will be so divided that it must succeed in its object. And when that happens, all you can do is accept your confusion and take what is left to you. For if you attempt to avert defeat with a series of inspired guesses, you will, as often as not, turn a minor calamity into a complete disaster.

Consider that simplest monkey wrench of all—the preemptive bid. Still easily the most effective of all nuisance bids. And the least dangerous to the user, provided it is made on reasonable playing strength. It mystifies nobody, partner knows exactly where he is, but it can put opponents in a very nasty spot merely because of the level from which it forces them to start operating.

Take a simple example. You hold:

(1) ♠ : 7 3
     ♡ : A K 8 5 2
     ◊ : A J 8 3
     ♣ : Q 5

And dealer, on your right, opens with three Spades. No getting away from it. You are in a spot.

Or again: You are South and hold:

(2) ♠ : K 7 6
     ♡ : 5
     ◊ : A K J 9 4 3
     ♣ : A 8 2

The bidding: North: One Club. East: Three Hearts.
Most annoying.

[101]

In Example (1) you can bid four Hearts. And you may make it or you may come an unholy cropper. Or you can pass and perhaps miss a Slam. Whatever you do you may get a filthy result.

The point to realize is this: abandon all hope of a scientifically reached par result. And decide what is your best hope now.

And in this case (Example 1) it is clearly to pass.

There are two more people to speak. They may clear up the situation. Even if they both pass it does not follow that you have missed four Hearts. Quite often you will find that you could not have made four Hearts, and they have not made three Spades.

Example (2) happened to me quite recently. Our opponents were not vulnerable. We were. It couldn't have been more infuriating. Instead of being able to bid two Diamonds over one Club and find our best contract in comfort (which might be anything from three No Trump to seven Diamonds), I had to take a stab in the dark. I nearly bid six Diamonds in a rage, but my early training prevailed. I conceded East full marks for the effectiveness of his nuisance bid, and settled down to find a bid that would give us the best possible result in light of that nuisance bid.

The obvious "safety first" bid was to double three Hearts. Clearly it was very unlikely that East could make it. Not impossible, but unlikely. The average expectancy for this double would be about 300 points.

But this was not good enough when there was an almost certain game and rubber, or a possible Slam in the hand for us. Furthermore, when East, who was a sensible player, bid three Hearts he was quite prepared to be doubled. He was expecting it.

And I hate doing what my opponents expect. And if, by any chance, three Hearts doubled should make—I just couldn't bear it.

Of course, if I could be guaranteed that my partner would dislike the double and take it out, that would be perfect. For then I should learn a bit more about my partner's hand, and that might tell me how to proceed.

But I had no such guarantee.

So, till I had considered all the other alternatives, the double was off.

I considered them.

Four Hearts? Out of the question. I was not nearly strong enough. That would be just asking for trouble.

Four Clubs? Five Clubs? Ridiculous! Partner might have a

four card suit. For a moment I toyed with the idea of four Diamonds. If my partner had opened on a maximum it would give him a chance to bid four No Trump, or even four Spades. In that case *I* could bid four No Trump. But I decided against it, for it was a greedy bid. It would work beautifully if partner had a maximum. But if he had opened on a minimum it might put him in an awful spot. He might even pass.

So I bid five Diamonds. It was far from perfect, but it was the best bid I could find. There should be a play for it whatever partner had opened on. And it told him at once, as no other bid could, that I was not stretching my hand to find a bid over the pre-empt, but that I had a darned good hand with a long and pretty solid Diamond suit. It still gave him the opportunity to bid six if he had opened on a maximum. And if there was a laydown Grand Slam, or, on the contrary, all the Diamonds were stacked against me—so that I went down at 5 Diamonds (whereas 5 or 6 Clubs could be made)—well there was nothing I could do about it.

Actually, North passed five Diamonds in a trance, and put down an absolute minimum: ♠ : 8, 4. ♡ : A, K, 7, 2. ◇ : 7, 6. ♣ : Q, J, 9, 6, 3. And I just scrambled home.

So it was all right. But it need not have been.

You will note that there are very few set rules of procedure in defending against pre-empts. Except in those rare cases where you hold such a whale of a hand that you can afford to bid the required number of No Trump over the pre-empt to force a response from your partner, you have to work out your own procedure each time. And all my experience has shown me that you get your best results in the long run by going quietly. Reasonable risks—yes; but not foolhardy risks—even if they do come off sometimes. A business double of a three Spade pre-empt on a balanced hand of about four honor tricks, which partner will take out if he has anything worth bidding, *and not otherwise*, is a reasonable risk. The number of times you will double them into game will be far less than the number of times you will get a good penalty, or else go game yourself.

When it comes to psychics, it is even more difficult to decide. For at least you do know all about a pre-emptive bid. But you don't know anything about a psychic—not even if it *is* one. But here I can suggest to you a method of procedure and a very excellent method, too. It is this:

Treat any suspected psychic as though it were a genuine bid and and bid your hand accordingly, until and unless proved otherwise.

And if the psychic isn't proved until the bidding is over, then stay psyched.

It is the same principle as that which applies against pre-emptive bids—a willingness to accept a bad result. A willingness to be psyched.

If you accept this, then quite often you may find your weren't. Let me tell you about the hand that finally taught me this.

It happened back in 1937 in the Metropolitan Pairs' Championship in New York, which, incidentally, I didn't win—or come even close. I was partnered by one of America's ranking players. And as long as the bidding was competitive—so that one had to play Bridge and not a system—we got along very nicely. But whenever we had the bidding to ourselves, we both adapted our bidding to please the other, got caught in a cross current and ended up in a series of contracts that would have disgraced a certified teacher. But that is by the way, and just to show that this "adapting" business can be overdone.

But now about the hand in question. Sitting South, I held the following:

♠ : K Q J 9 7 6
♡ : K J 7 6
◇ : A Q 5
♣ : None

We were vulnerable, our opponents were not. West dealt and passed. North passed. East bid one Spade.

Now East was one of America's leading players, a winner of many tournaments, and, most disturbing of all, famed for his psychic bidding. We were vulnerable. He wasn't. He had opened third hand.

It couldn't have been more suspicious.

However, the one thing you should not do in Bridge is to think for half an hour and then pass. Not because it is unethical—that only happens when your partner takes advantage of it—but because it gives the show away to the opponents. So I had no time to think the matter out. I passed.

West bid two No Trump. This, of course, confirmed my suspicion that East had psyched. If West had enough strength to bid two No Trump, and I had my whale of a hand, what could East have? The answer was almost certainly a long suit of Clubs, into which he was going to switch if doubled.

North passed. East bid three Hearts.

As I had passed one Spade there was clearly no point in bidding now. I passed again.

West bid three No Trump. North passed. East passed.

[104]

And there I was.

Now I had time to think. I was still certain East had psyched, and would switch into Clubs if doubled. But that was not the point. Were we missing anything ourselves? Could we make four Spades? There was just no answer to that one. We might or we might not. West evidently had a fairly good hand. My partner had passed. It was a pure toss-up.

The next point was, could they make four Clubs? Probably not, but they might not be set many—certainly not as many as they would be at three No Trump. Should I pass and let them play three No Trump undoubled? If they went down five it might still be a fair result. But again no—for if I did not double, my partner was almost certain to lead a Club, of which he probably held something like J, x, x, x, and they might even make their contract.

So, almost reluctantly, and with many misgivings, I doubled. I still had not decided what I would do if East bid four Clubs.

West tranced, clearly contemplating a re-double, then passed. North passed.

East passed.

North led the ten of Spades. We defeated that contract six tricks = 1100 points.

The four hands were:

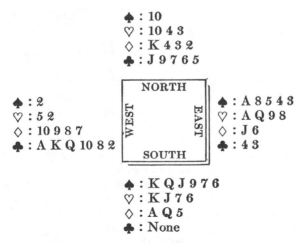

♠ : 10
♡ : 10 4 3
♢ : K 4 3 2
♣ : J 9 7 6 5

NORTH
WEST
EAST
SOUTH

♠ : 2
♡ : 5 2
♢ : 10 9 8 7
♣ : A K Q 10 8 2

♠ : A 8 5 4 3
♡ : A Q 9 8
♢ : J 6
♣ : 4 3

♠ : K Q J 9 7 6
♡ : K J 7 6
♢ : A Q 5
♣ : None

West, not East, was the psychist. East merely had a very weak opening bid, and had rather unwisely bid the hand twice, trying to find a safe landing spot.

East put up the Ace of Spades. He could see eight tricks, provided the Clubs broke, and the hope for some sort of an end

[105]

play for the ninth. As the Clubs didn't break, and as he took the Heart finesse to try and save something from the wreck, he went down six. A cold top for us.

For at all the other tables, and there were twenty-five of them, South's hand had got busy over East's bid of one Spade, and N.-S. had ended up in a series of Spade contracts ranging up to four Spades redoubled. The next best result to ours was a pair that had somehow got themselves into three No Trump, which (as their opponents forgot to cash their five tricks) they made. But that only scored 600 points.

It boiled down to this: I couldn't have been more wrong about the hand while it was being bid. I couldn't have got a better result.

Blind luck? I sat down to think it out. I found that, quite unconsciously I had stumbled on the right principle of defense against psychics—the principle of believing them, pending further evidence. By my willingness to be psyched, I had given our opponents plenty of rope to hang themselves, and they had.

And the fact that on this occasion East-West were only semi-psychic did not affect the principle of my discovery.

The hand is a trap for either side. And the hand had trapped the opponents, not us, because I had bid my own values in accordance with the bidding and ignored my suspicions. For it is clear that if the bid of one Spade is genuine, then my only possible bid is to pass awaiting developments. There is no other sensible bid to make at this stage.

But suppose East had been bidding a psychic? Would not my beautiful top have become a bottom?

The answer is, not necessarily. The subsequent bidding might have revealed the psychic and allowed us to find our correct contract. Or not. Or, quite likely, opponents would get into so much trouble with their psychic that it would more than compensate us for anything we might have missed.

For, when I passed one Spade there was nothing to make East suspect that his partner's bid was not genuine.

For the man who bids a psychic shoots a very dangerous arrow into the air, and his partner will have an awful time trying to follow it if the opposition remains silent and refuses to point out his path to him.

Therefore I urge you to forget that there is such a thing as a psychic in the opening round of bidding. Treat the suspected bid as genuine. Make the normal bid over it. If you have an informatory double make it. If you have the values to overbid with one No Trump, bid one No Trump. And if policy dictates a pass, then pass.

Of course, sometimes the remaining cards will be distributed in such a manner that the psychic will remain undiscovered until too late and you will get a bad result. That is inevitable. But you will find that this policy will expose a large percentage of the psychics without at any time running any appreciable risk yourself. When it doesn't, the opponents will get into trouble quite a lot of the time.

And, final argument, you will gain heavily each time opponents are not psychic. For then they will be landed with the misfit hand instead of you.

Now a very necessary word of warning. The bulk of the points won at Bridge is won by finding your own correct contract and not by pushing the enemy into the wrong one. It is only when the enemy nuisance bidding has made it too difficult for you to reach your own contract, except by guessing, that you should fall back on the secondary objective.

So do not allow the policy of passing good hands because there is nothing better to do develop into a policy of trap passes on enormous holdings in the hope that the enemy will get into trouble. They won't do it often enough. And, on balance, it can only result in a loss of bidding time and unnecessary difficulties later.

Whenever you have an obvious, sound, constructive bid to make, don't wait. Make it. Don't worry whether the enemy are psychic, semi-psychic, riding for a fall, or just plumb crazy.

Make it.

Tell your partner about your hand.

Go after your own contract.

CHAPTER

TEN

Fixed—By Palookas!

THE TITLE of this chapter is taken from an article that appeared in the *American Bridge World* some years ago. Most of the arguments come from Culbertson's *Blue Book*.

No matter. Maybe the phrasing will be different.

The article described a rubber between two very clever experts and two honest palookas. Smacking their lips over the appetizing meal offered to them, the two experts cut loose with an orgy of psychics that should have reduced their stupid opponents to a helpless bewilderment and fooled them out of all the good hands they kept on getting. But their stupid opponents were far too unimaginative to be fooled. They just looked at their cards and bid them stolidly. And as the rubber progressed and the experts took penalty after penalty, their frenzy increased and their psychics grew wilder until they were fooling each other and ended up by playing a lay-down Grand Slam in a part score contract because each thought the other was psyching. And the next hand they were too sulky to psych any more; and the stolid palookas bid a stolid three No Trump, made it, and won an enormous rubber.

The experts paid up but made no attempt to look pleasant about it.

Now, the experts fully deserved their loss. They had a natural advantage in skill over their opponents. But, by adopting the tactics they did, they threw their advantage out of the window, and, halfway through the rubber, had become the worse pair of the two.

Because they had stopped trying to make the best of their own cards and were concentrating all their energies on trying to lure the palookas into making the worst of theirs.

And it just can't be done—against palookas. You can't bluff a palooka out of his heritage. He might dissipate it all by himself, but he won't be bluffed out of it.

Because nothing will persuade a palooka that he holds a bad hand when he thinks he holds a good one.

You've a far better chance of persuading *me*!

For, at least, I know all the snags a good hand can contain. And if your psyching is well enough timed, you might persuade me that the dangers are too great to go on bidding.

But you will never persuade a palooka. He cannot see the dangers of a good hand. He can only see the Aces and Kings.

That's why he is a palooka.

That's why he accepts such tremendous penalties when the dangers are real.

And that's why he will sock you every time you try to frighten him with imaginary ones.

You can't psych a palooka. He's far too dense.

Besides, it's so unnecessary.

As Richard Lederer wrote: "There is no need to psych against weak opponents. They are quite capable of getting into trouble without your assistance."

You have three natural advantages over the palooka. You play your dummies better, you defend better, and you bid better. Quite enough to go on with when you sit down with a pet partner against a pair of them. Quite enough to make you assured winners in the long run.

But not nearly enough to assure that you will win this particular rubber.

And that is the whole point.

In spite of all your skill, the palookas must win an occasional rubber. When you have resigned yourself to accepting this monstrous injustice when it occurs and stop throwing away thousands in futile efforts to prevent it, you will revert to your rightful status as the better pair.

But as long as you continue to try to psych the palookas out of every contract, I'll back the palookas.

Of course, you can take certain liberties. You can overbid your hand slightly, knowing that you are unlikely to get the best defense. You can make dangerous over-calls for palookas don't double low level contracts. And you can double more freely yourself, for palookas don't often redouble and quite often misplay their hands. But all this is merely a little bit of jam to go with the butter.

But you won't get any jam if you overdo it.

Give your natural advantages a chance and you will win many rubbers to which you are not entitled.

But not all of them.

And as long as you continue to try and win all of them, I'll back the palookas.

While I was writing this chapter, I played a rubber with a palooka against stronger opposition. At any rate, they considered themselves stronger.

We won a forty-seven-hundred-point rubber.

Certainly we had the cards to win the rubber. But equally certainly we did not have the cards to win forty-seven hundred points. That was just a gift from opponents who could not bear to lose a rubber.

Almost the whole thing might have happened as an illustration.

This is how it went.

On the first hand our opponents bid and made a game. On the second hand my palooka went down in a game he could have made. He was an honest palooka and, within his limitations, quite sound; but the hand was just too difficult for him. My mistake—for putting him into it.

Feeling well on top now, our opponents stuck their necks out on the next hand and I socked them for 500 points. This annoyed them a little and they said a few words to each other.

And now catastrophe came to our opponents. We bid and made a Grand Slam. There were eighteen cold tricks in the combined hands. A pair of infants could have bid it; and made it.

The injustice of the inferior pair picking up such a hand hurt the opponents. They brooded over it all through the next hand, which I played at one No Trump; and, instead of going down one, I made two.

Next hand our opponents picked up the following:

Dealer West.

The bidding proceeded as follows:

WEST	NORTH	EAST	SOUTH (Me)
Pass	Pass	1 ◇	1 ♡
1 ♠	2 ♡	Pass	3 ♡
Pass	Pass	4 ♣	Pass
Pass	Double		All pass

Study the bidding of the opponents. Apart from the opening bid, of which I personally approve, it is desperation bidding of the worst type. The perpetrators themselves could not disapprove more strongly in theory of the bids they made in practice. But they made them because they were losing a large rubber to an inferior pair and just couldn't bear it. And in that mood there is no judgment left—only panic.

However, with a normal division of Clubs, four Clubs doubled, does not appear such a bad contract. But the Trumps were divided 4–0, and I sat with A, J, 8, x, x, of Diamonds over the declarer. In addition, West played the hand for miracles—hoping to get out with two down—and succeeded in going down five.

Another 1400 for us.

Incidentally it is very doubtful if we could have made three Hearts. Certainly not with a trump lead.

My partner now dealt and bid one Heart. I held the following:

♠ : 10 8 6 5 2
♡ : K Q 10 7
◇ : None
♣ : A J 9 5

We were certainly getting all the cards. One always does in this type of rubber. That is why, when it happens against you, it is so much better to go quietly.

Opponents did not go quietly. East bid two Diamonds.

I made a waiting bid of three Hearts. True, this gave us game, but I knew opponents weren't passing in the present atmosphere.

West bid four Diamonds. North bid four Hearts. Interesting!

East bid five Diamonds. A very prompt five Diamonds.

I bid six Hearts.

I did not know whether we could, or could not, make it. And I didn't care. For by now it was of technical interest only. Because by now we were so well on top and our opponents so demoralized that I was absolutely certain they would not let us play it. They would bid seven Diamonds.

They did—and went down 1100 points.

As a point of technical interest six Hearts couldn't have been

[111]

made with the lead of a singleton Spade from East, West holding the Ace.

We now got another rock-crusher, and, with opponents utterly deflated, made a peaceful two No Trump to clinch the rubber.

Fixed—by palookas? Or by themselves?

I leave it to you.

Now let us consider the situation the other way round. Let us suppose you are one of the palookas playing against two experts. What should your tactics be?

Of course, if the experts are behaving in the manner I have just described, you won't need any. But if they insist on playing a sound, steady game, then it's more difficult. The odds are against you winning.

Should you try and win? Or should you concentrate on losing the minimum?

If you try to win and fail, you will lose a lot more points than you would have done if you had played steady Bridge. An awful lot more points.

So forget it and concentrate on losing the minimum. Just as you did with Mrs. Guggenheim. Though the situation is not so hopeless, the principle is the same.

This, of course, does not apply to Duplicate Bridge, where all that matters is winning, and there is no financial difference whether you lose the match by ten points or by ten thousand. Then it is no use at all playing a sound and steady game, for the opponents will be sounder and steadier than you are. You may lose the match by a smaller margin; but you will still lose it. No, just as there is no need for the stronger team to play "fancy stuff" against weaker opponents, so the inferior team must play fancy if it is to have any chance at all.

In the first place, as I have already point out, a strong player is more easily psyched than a weak one. In the second place it will take the strong team a long time to realize that you have had the impertinence to try and psych them. THEM! When they do realize it, they might be tempted to retaliate and allow the match to develop into a glorious free-for-all guessing contest with skill at a discount and swings of thousands either way. And anything might happen then.

Of course, in most cases, you will lose the match by some stupendous margin. So what! You'd have lost it, anyway. As well be hanged for a sheep as for a goat. And you'll have had a lot of fun without even paying for it.

And just once in a while all the luck will be in your favor and you'll win.

But that is Duplicate.

In rubber Bridge, you just can't afford such luxuries. It's too expensive to score off experts once in a while and lose huge rubbers the rest of the time.

You must aim at losing the minimum.

So when you are up against it, concentrate almost entirely on the plus side of your score. Be satisfied to pile it up in small amounts. Whenever you have a close decision about a bid, select the one that *must* give you a plus score however it turns out. The bid which, though it may not give you the best result on the hand, will at any rate give you a plus result.

A certain game rather than a doubtful slam.

And, much more important and less obvious, *a certain part score rather than a doubtful game.*

Because part scores can total up into a game. A great many Bridge players don't seem to know this, but they can.

No doubt you can remember many rubbers where you bid four games in succession and went down in all of them. That made your score somewhere around minus 200. Had you taken four part scores, you would have won a thousand-point rubber. That's a swing of 1200 points on part scores.

Remember a rubber like that? I do. Plenty of them.

In any circumstances it is folly to despise part scores. Against stronger opposition, it is lunacy.

Even assuming that none of your part scores get converted into games or yield any penalties, the swings contained in the part scores themselves will help a great deal towards your objective of keeping the rubber small. Three Spades bid and made scores 90 points. Four Spades bid, and one down loses 50 points. That is a swing of 140 points. Two or three such swings in a rubber total quite a respectable amount.

And against that, with all the added possibilities of conversion and penalties, all you lose will be the doubtful games that, as it turns out, you could have made if you had shot for them. And there won't be so many of them.

There never are—against a good defense.

So it boils down to this:

When you are the better pair—don't under-rate your opponents. Loosen up on your bidding when it is safe, but in the main, rely on your superior skill. Don't try to push opponents into mistakes—let them make them for themselves.

When you are the weaker pair—go quietly. Concentrate on keeping your losing rubbers small, and rely on getting more than your share of the good cards for the winning ones.

Of course, rely on the contempt of your opponents. On no

account do anything to decrease that contempt. For the more contemptuous they get, the more it will seem to them an outrage that you should score any points at all. And the more likely they are to take one liberty too many.

And that, as I have shown, is your best chance.

Loosen up your bidding against weak defense. Tighten up against good defense. Here, as a practical example to end this chapter, is a very ordinary near-slam hand.

You are North and hold:

♠ : A K x x x
♡ : K 10 x x
◇ : A K J
♣ : x

The bidding, with opponents silent, proceeds:

NORTH	SOUTH
1 ♠	3 ♠
4 N.T.*	5 ♣
5 ◇	5 ♠

Partner has shown the Ace of Clubs to your first slam try but refused to bid six Spades over your second slam try.

You know that you are missing the Ace of Hearts. Also it is almost certain that your partner does not hold a singleton Heart or even the Queen of Hearts, for surely in that case he could have bid six Spades.

What should you do?

The answer depends on the caliber of the opponent on your left.

If he is a good defensive player, you pass. Because there is an even money chance of the Ace of Hearts sitting over the King and if that is the case, the slam will almost certainly not be there.

But if East is a bad defensive player, you bid six Spades. Because if he has the Ace of Hearts, the chances are in favor of his leading it.

The North hand above was held by Adam Meredith. I was his partner and held:

♠ : Q J 9 x
♡ : x x x
◇ : Q 10
♣ : A Q J x

_____
*Not Blackwood.

[114]

Meredith knew that I was not chary of bidding up weak hands. He knew that if I refused to contract for Six Spades I had a reason. But he also knew the opponent on his left. So he bid six Spades. And sure enough the opponent promptly led out the Ace of Hearts, and the slam became a lay-down.

That is why I rate Meredith as one of the best money players in the country.

CHAPTER ELEVEN

The Logic of Luck

THERE IS no paradox about the title of this chapter. Luck has no logic. But there is no reason not to be logical about luck.

Very few Bridge players are.

Very few Bridge players have any views about luck at all, beyond moaning about it when it is bad and attributing the results to their superior skill when it is good.

They have never thought about luck.

That is why this chapter is necessary.

Bridge is primarily a game of luck and only secondarily a game of skill. Before you jump to dispute this, consider a single deal. The way the cards are dealt is pure luck. Skill only enters after the deal, and even then, as you know, it is not always rewarded. Appalling contracts succeed. Legitimate contracts get heavily penalized.

It depends how the luck is running.

It is only because in the long run luck evens itself out that skill becomes the predominant factor and the skilled player must win from the unskilled.

But that is in the long run.

In the short run, luck dominates the issue. Which is why two palookas can win a rubber against two experts.

And which is why the way your own luck is running must always be considered if you want to win at Bridge.

Or at anything else.

Luck levels itself out in the long run. But there is no orderly process about the leveling. The patches of good, bad, phenomenal, shocking and "never seen anything like it!" luck do not supersede each other in a nice orderly sequence. Most of the time they are all jumbled together so that no particular pattern can be identified.

This is known as luck running even.

But from time to time a particular patch will last a little longer and begin to dominate the other patches. And then the pattern can be identified and labeled. And so you get lucky seats and lucky cards, players in form and players out of form.

Now, while there is no telling how long any particular pattern will last, there is no mistaking it while it is lasting. And while it lasts it is, in my opinion, folly to ignore it.

Luck has no logic.

There is no reason why high cards should continue to be directed to certain seats. But, while it is happening, it seems to me perfectly logical to try and sit in one of them.

And the logic of all the other patterns of luck, including your own personal pattern, is equally indisputable.

If you are in luck—play more.

If you are out of luck—play less.

But the majority of card players, the very same players who believe in lucky seats, lucky cards and turning their chair round three times, do just the opposite. Whereas on the extraneous patterns, they carry to exaggeration their attempts to play with the luck, in all their personal patterns they insist on playing against it.

To confirm this you have only to study the late games at your club. They are invariably made up of all the losers of the evening—the players who are out of luck. The only exceptions will be the club professionals cashing in on the bad luck of the others.

The winners have gone home satisfied. Had they been losers, out of luck, they would have been playing on. But as their luck was good they have gone home.

In every club there are players who will only make up a late game if they are losing. And, when the proprietor is looking happy around midnight, it means that they are losing. It is not that he wishes them any harm, but late games are very profitable to a club.

It is, of course, very tempting to behave illogically about your personal luck. Luck may change, and it is very tempting to hang on to your winnings. Luck may change, and it is even more tempting to play on and get back your losses. Especially as, sometimes, it does change and you do get them back. More often, though, it doesn't and you merely turn an average loss into a heavy one.

I have practically conquered the first temptation—to stop

[116]

when I am winning. I wait for concrete evidence that my run
of luck is exhausting itself before getting up from the table.
Two consecutive rubbers lost. Cast iron contracts wrecked by
unlucky distributions. And so on. And I never begrudge the
points I give back waiting for this evidence. For quite often I
have won half-a-dozen or more rubbers before losing the warn-
ing-off two, and turned a very nice win into a superb one.

But I have not yet entirely conquered the temptation to
play on when I'm losing. And, in spite of the occasional re-
coveries, it costs me a lot of money each year. But at least
when I succumb to this temptation I know that I am doing it
and I curse myself even as I succumb.

But the majority of offenders seem to be under the impression that they are doing the right thing.

And a principle that causes you to play more rubbers "out
of luck" than "in" cannot be right.

I do not expect you to be able to conquer this temptation all
the time any more than I can. But, once you are aware that the
principle is wrong, you may conquer it some of the time.

It is natural to want to play on when you are losing. But to
plan to do so is just plain lunacy.

He was a very minor and unpretentious professional playing
in a suburban club where the stakes were a tenth of a cent.
And he worked out for himself, poor soul, what he thought was
a nice safe way of making a steady income. Nothing ambitious.
He set himself out to win just five dollars a day. *Five dollars*
every day. The moment he had won his five dollars he would
stop playing. He did this very comfortably for several months.
Sometimes he was out of the club within an hour after coming
into it. Sometimes it took longer. But, for some time, it worked
very nicely and he felt very pleased with himself. Idiot.

Came the inevitable run of bad luck and he could not go
home nice and early. So he toiled through the night with the
cards running against him and he got up in the morning out
twenty-five dollars.

He took it philosophically. These things happened.

But it happened again the next day. And the day after that.
And when he had lost over $150 playing day and night his
bad run came to an end and he started once again to win his
$5 a day and getting home nice and early.

And then he hit another bad run of luck and lost at the rate of
$25 a day until it was over.

"Would you believe it," he said to me, "among all those
rabbits I could only just show a profit for the year."

[117]

When I told him that in that company he ought to average $100 a week in comfort, he shook his head and said that he had been much less ambitious than that. And he explained his system. And when I explained to him what a fool he was he couldn't see it and went off muttering something about "my luck must turn."

A hopeless case. Of all the silly systems in existence he had chosen the silliest. And he proposed to continue with it in the hope that his luck would turn.

But his system is specifically devised to give luck no chance of turning.

Consider the thing from first principles. The average Bridge player's luck runs in patches, which, in the long run, average up to make him averagely lucky. If he fails to exploit his good runs he must be a loser on luck.

But our professional's system expressly forbade him to exploit his good runs. For, directly he had won $5, it told him to stop playing.

So that on the days his luck was in and he had won his $5 in three or four rubbers, he waved luck good-by and went home.

And on the days that his luck was average, which meant that with his advantage in skill he was going to win comfortably, he also went home when he had won his $5.

It was only on the days when his luck was dead out that he went on playing.

Which meant that, under this system, the majority of his time at the card table was spent when he was out of luck.

What chance had he got?

There is yet another reason why it is advisable to stop playing when you are out of luck. A most logical reason. I offer it for the consideration of all those players who do not believe in continued patterns of luck continuing, and play on obstinately with the cards spitting at them.

Unless you are a very rare exception, a bad run will influence your judgment and render you incapable of producing your best game. So that if a slice of luck does come your way, the chances are that you will fail to take advantage of it.

I can stand up to a bad run of luck rather better than the next man; but I do not begin to claim that my game is unaffected. I lose boldness, I miss opportunities, I fail to find just that little bit extra that makes all the difference. And if I go on playing too long on any one day I begin to make baby mistakes and mess up contracts that normally I could make in my sleep.

[118]

Here is an example taken from a bad run of luck I had only too recently:

♠ : J 10 9 8 7
♡ : A K Q 4
◇ : 7 3
♣ : A J

```
┌─────────────────┐
│     NORTH       │
│  W           E  │
│  E           A  │
│  S           S  │
│  T           T  │
│     SOUTH       │
└─────────────────┘
```

♠ : A K Q 6
♡ : 5
◇ : A Q 8 2
♣ : Q 6 5 4

I was South. It was the second deal of the rubber and we were vulnerable. The contract was six Spades and the opening lead was the nine of Hearts, which I won with the Ace.

Now the contract is cold against any defense and any distribution. But, with great care, I played the hand as follows:

At trick two I played a small Heart and trumped with the Ace of Spades. So far—perfect.

I then played the King of Spades and West showed out. I draw the remaining trumps, ending in dummy. I played a small Diamond and finessed the Queen! It lost.

A Club was led. I finessed the Jack. It lost.

One down.

Just my luck! A contract depending on one of two finesses and both wrong!

And it was not till somebody pointed it out that it dawned on me that the Diamond finesse was unnecessary. All I had to do was to play Ace of Clubs, followed by Jack of Clubs and chuck Dummy's losing Diamond on my Queen of Clubs.

I just hadn't seen it!

I was in a bad run of luck. I have been in a bad run for some weeks and it had reached its crescendo at this session with a loss of over ten thousand points in under two hours. On the surface my game was still normal. I wasn't making any noticeably bad bids, I wasn't bidding hopeless slams just to get something back, and I wasn't indulging in prolific, senseless sacrifices. But neither was I making any good bids, or finding the

[119]

one Killer lead to defeat opposing contracts. My game had gone wooden. And now, with this hand, it had degenerated into a spectacular debacle.

Instead of winning a seventeen rubber I eventually lost a twelve.

At this point I did have the sense to get up and leave.

Later on, in a calmer frame of mind, I reviewed the session I had played. There was nothing else in it so expensive as the swing of twenty-nine hundred points in the rubber I have described; but there were several minor mistakes, such as handing our opponents a part score, which later enabled them to go game; and there were several cheap sacrifices I might have made and hadn't. What was even worse, there were two hands, which at the time I had dismissed as "Unlucky. Wrong guess," that, on further inspection, offered a cast-iron line of play that I had completely overlooked. So had everybody else at the inquest. But that was hardly a consolation. Adding it all up I found that I had thrown away just under 10,000 points. So, had I been playing at my best, my enormous losing session would have been a small loss only.

And I am a seasoned veteran.

This confession does not contradict my statement that in a bad run of luck I am rather better than the next man. It only emphasizes how bad the next man can be.

At least in an unlucky streak I merely play badly. The next man is very apt to play hysterically.

It has been said that you cannot judge the real caliber of a Bridge player until you have seen him in a losing run.

I agree.

You have only to watch the habitual good card-holders on the rare occasions when the cards desert them. They may be first-class winning players, but let them lose four or five rubbers in succession, and their skill flies out of the window and they lose about three times as much as they need to. They are so used to holding big hands that they are quite unadapted to cope with a series of bad ones. It is a pleasure to watch one of them paying up with the slightly dazed expression of a person who cannot believe that this thing has really happened.

The slightly under-average card-holder is better off. He is used to bad cards and can stand up to a bad run for much longer before the effects of it become apparent in his play. But he too has his limit.

In fact, if there is a Bridge or Poker player who remains entirely unaffected by a prolonged bad run, I have yet to meet him.

[120]

It is quite clear now, I trust, why you should plan to play the maximum when you are in luck and the minimum when you are out of it.

As it is impossible, or at any rate legally impossible, to arrange to play in luck all the time, that minimum is unavoidable. For though you can, and should, cut down your Bridge during a bad run, you must nevertheless play a certain amount, or you will never know when it is over. You can, of course, give up Bridge altogether, but that solution is only for the consistently unlucky.

For the ordinary average card-holder there is nothing to do but to play out his bad run and endeavor not to lose too much while it lasts.

Let me see if I can help you achieve this. The fact that I am frequently unable to follow my own advice is no argument against its soundness.

We have seen that the chief danger in a bad run of luck is the effect on your morale: and the consequent deterioration in your play. Therefore, the first essential in combating a bad run is to devise some method of keeping your morale as high as possible.

The effects of bad luck on morale are cumulative. Lose one rubber and the effect is negligible. Lose three or four and you begin to get depressed. Lose a dozen in succession in one session and you will reach a state of gloom where you feel you have lost the thirteenth even before you have started it. And then you will lose it for a certainty, for you will undoubtedly muck up any chance you get of winning it.

Now a rest from the Bridge table breaks up that cumulative effect and brings you back nearer to normal. You may have lost every rubber the preceding day, but after a night's sleep you will sit down at the card table once again hopeful of winning.

Let me put it another way. If you have lost twenty rubbers in succession the effect on your morale will be much less if you have lost them, say, in four sessions rather than in one.

Therefore, your first resolve during a bad run must be not to play too many rubbers in any one session. About five rubbers is ample. If your luck is still out—call it a day then. Or, if you cannot bring yourself to achieve that, then, at least, cut out for a couple of rubbers and watch. Even that short break will restore you a little.

As for your actual play during a bad run there are many schools of thought. Personally, I believe that you should, as nearly as possible, play your normal game—with the one exception of never giving yourself the benefit of the doubt. If a game, or a slam, is worth bidding, bid it. If a sacrifice is worth while, make it. Do not deliberately underbid merely because you are out of luck. It is just as foolish to turn ultra-conservative as ultra-reckless.

On the border line hands, however, I do think it will pay you to pull in a notch. For instance, a small slam, depending on a King finesse, which you may shoot for freely when you are in luck, should now be avoided. If you are out of luck, it's more likely to be wrong. But a small slam depending on one of two finesses should still be bid. To refrain would be overdoing it.

Similarly, in sacrifice bidding, against even opposition, you should still be prepared to pay 300 points to save a rubber. Never mind if you feel it will only result in their getting a slam on the next hand. You cannot pander to your feelings to quite that extent.

On the other hand, if your hand is such that you cannot foretell whether your sacrifice is going to be cheap or not, refrain. Just as when you are in luck, bid.

For instance, sitting West, not vulnerable against vulnerable opponents, you hold:

♠ : J x x
♡ : A J 10 x x x
◇ : x
♣ : K J x

North deals and the bidding proceeds as follows:

NORTH	EAST	SOUTH	WEST
Pass	Pass	1 ♣	1 ♡
1 ♠	2 ♡	4 ♠	?

Now, this is a tantalizing situation, for the key to the hand is with East and East's holding is wrapt in mystery.

True he has raised Hearts but that still leaves too many variations to enable you to reach any definite conclusions. All you know at the moment is, that if he has the right cards, a sacrifice will be very cheap. And, if he has the wrong ones, such as strength in Diamonds, the sacrifice may be dear, with the added annoyance that in that case four Spades will probably not make. There is also the strong probability that he has a singleton Spade, but as North has bid Spades at the one level that is not a certainty.

The best course, with a good partner, is to pass and let him tackle the problem. But one has not always got a good partner. And when the hand happened to me—I hadn't. But, on the other hand, I was playing strictly in form. So I bid five Hearts, expecting it to cost about 300 points but hoping it might only cost one hundred. North doubled—I can't think why—and all passed.

It turned out that East's hand was nearly worth a raise to three Hearts; and I made the contract, for the four hands were:

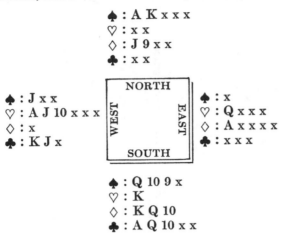

♠ : A K x x x
♡ : x x
◇ : J 9 x x
♣ : x x

WEST
♠ : J x x
♡ : A J 10 x x x
◇ : x
♣ : K J x

EAST
♠ : x
♡ : Q x x x
◇ : A x x x x
♣ : x x x

SOUTH
♠ : Q 10 9 x
♡ : K
◇ : K Q 10
♣ : A Q 10 x x

I lost only a Club and a Spade. Incidentally, on a Diamond ruff North must go down one at four Spades.

Still, it was a very fine result. But then I was playing in luck.

Had I been playing out of luck, however, nothing would have induced me to bid five Hearts. For, on the bidding, there was no reason at all why the four hands might not have been, say:

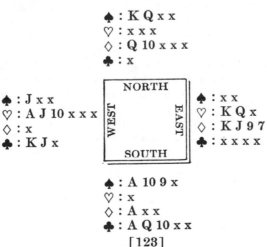

♠ : K Q x x
♡ : x x x
◇ : Q 10 x x x
♣ : x

WEST
♠ : J x x
♡ : A J 10 x x x
◇ : x
♣ : K J x

EAST
♠ : x x
♡ : K Q x
◇ : K J 9 7
♣ : x x x x

SOUTH
♠ : A 10 9 x
♡ : x
◇ : A x x
♣ : A Q 10 x x

[123]

In this case 5 Hearts goes down four and 4 Spades, against careful defense, is still not makable.

It is true I have constructed this last hand. But there is nothing particularly abnormal about it. And, when you are out of luck, this is the sort of thing that keeps on happening to you.

CHAPTER

TWELVE

A Rubber at the Club

THIS RUBBER was never played.

But all the hands in it were.

Several of the hands are taken from one rubber and, in many cases, the sequences happened as shown.

I have had to give up my original idea of taking some interesting rubber and reproducing it here hand by hand. I could not find a single rubber in which all the hands were worth reproducing. There were many with mistakes made on every hand, but invariably these were hands not worth reproducing merely to comment on the mistake. And once I admitted the necessity of departing from actual event it was only common sense to depart a little further and select my hands from many rubbers in order to make this one as interesting as possible.

I have made up a foursome of players, three of whom you have already met in this book, and presented the hands so that their bidding and play remain in character. The characters are fictitious, but the hands are real.

You will agree with me, that they form the sort of spectacular but by no means unique group that might occur at your club at any time.

Certainly they might at mine.

The Players

North.　The Unlucky Expert

South.　Mrs. Guggenheim

West.　Mr. Smug

East.　Futile Willie

You have not yet met Futile Willie in this book, though you have met him at your club. He is a very bad good player. Theoretically he is almost in the expert class. But since he lacks any kind of judgment there is such a general futility about his tactics that he loses almost as much as Mrs. Guggenheim.

Preliminaries

"Forcing two, partner?" asked Futile Willie.
"Why not?" said Mr. Smug.
"Strong No Trump?"
"More or less," agreed Mr. Smug.
"Culbertson Four-Five?"
"Blackwood," said Smug firmly.

"Two Club, partner?" quavered Mrs. Guggenheim.
The Unlucky Expert looked at her. "I suppose so," he said disgusted.

DEAL NO. 1

West dealer. Neither side vulnerable.

♠ : J 10 x
♡ : A x x
◊ : x x
♣ : A x x x x

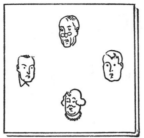

♠ : K Q x x
♡ : Q 10 x x x
◊ : A J 9 x
♣ : None

♠ : A x x
♡ : K
◊ : Q 10 x x
♣ : K J 10 9 8

♠ : x x x
♡ : J x x x
◊ : K x x
♣ : Q x x

The bidding:

WEST	NORTH	EAST	SOUTH
Pass	Pass	1♣	Pass
1♡	Pass	2♣	Pass
2♠	Pass	2 NT	Pass
3◊ (a)	Pass	4◊ (b)	Pass
5◊ (c)	Pass	6◊ (d)	Pass
Pass	Pass		

(a) So far, Mr. Smug has bid his hand surprisingly well. With this bid he has completed a very accurate picture. He has shown that he holds five Hearts, four Spades and four Diamonds and that he has fair but no overwhelming strength as he has not made a forcing bid at any stage.

(b) Just about what the hand is worth.

(c) Mr. Smug bids one more for game.

(d) A typical Futile Willie lunacy. He begins by bidding four Diamonds, which is not forcing, and when partner, who might well be stretching his hand, bids game, he decides that his hand is now worth a slam. This means in effect that the hand can be played at four Diamonds or at six Diamonds, but never at five Diamonds.

[126]

The obvious course for Willie, if he felt his hand was slammish, which it wasn't, was to bid five Diamonds at once, which would have combined an invitation to slam with the possibility of playing in game.

The Play

The Unlucky Expert pondered for a long time over his lead. Prospects looked poor—in spite of the bidding. His Spade holding suggested that the suit would break, his doubleton Diamond made it probable that any Diamond finesse would be right for declarer, and his Ace of Clubs was clearly not going to make. Desperation measures were called for. And he made a really excellent shot.

He led a small Club.

This was his reasoning. He has one trick—the Ace of Hearts. The only prospect of another trick appears to be in trumps. The bidding has made it clear that the enemy trumps are divided four-four. Therefore, his partner has three trumps and one of them might be the King. If the Ace of trump is with East, the contract is defeated anyway. But if this Ace is with West, then partner's King will be finessed . . .

Unless West can be forced to ruff twice and thus reduce his holding to two trumps.

To do this the Club suit must be attacked. If Dummy's Clubs are as good as King-Queen, then this plan will fail. But it will do no harm for there is nothing of value in West's hand to discard on one Club. But if Dummy's Clubs are King, Jack, and he fails to play the King, then the plan will work. So North opened the four of Clubs.

Mr. Smug did not give the matter a moment's thought. Who on earth would underlead an Ace against a slam contract? He played the Jack.

Mrs. Guggenheim hovered agonized. Who on earth would underlead an Ace against a slam contract? She pulled out the Queen of Clubs. She put it back. She pulled it out again. The Unlucky Expert gritted his teeth. She played it.

Of course, it had not yet occurred to Mr. Smug that he was in trouble. "No Clubs, partner," he announced, trumping the Queen with gusto.

He now inspected the hand. Even his cheerful optimism blanched a little.

"One or two things got to be right," he conceded and led a Heart.

The Unlucky Expert won with the Ace and played the Ace of Clubs.

"Oh," said Mr. Smug, just about to trump it. Then he realized this would leave him with only two trumps. He tranced.

But eventually it occurred to him that if he did not trump it he was down one anyway. So reluctantly he parted with his nine of Diamonds.

The Unlucky Expert relaxed. That trance had told him all he wanted to know: his partner held the King and two small Diamonds. He leaned back purring at his own cleverness.

But he purred too soon. Mr. Smug entered dummy by ruffing a Heart, and led the Queen of Diamonds. Without a trace of hesitation, Mrs. Guggenheim covered!

Always cover an honor with an honor. Had not the Unlucky Expert told her this only two rubbers back?

"I felt it ought to be a slam," said Futile Willie happily. "You see, I knew you had no Clubs."

"Had to play it right," said Mr. Smug, puffing at his pipe.

"We couldn't defeat it—could we?" said Mrs. Guggenheim anxiously. She did not care about the loss. She only wanted to be absolved from blame.

"No," said the Unlucky Expert sadly. *"We* couldn't."

Points chucked by North-South

620+300 for game+50 (down one, not vulnerable). Total 970.

The Score Sheet

N—S	E—W
═══	500
	═══
	120

DEAL NO. 2

North deals. East-West vulnerable.

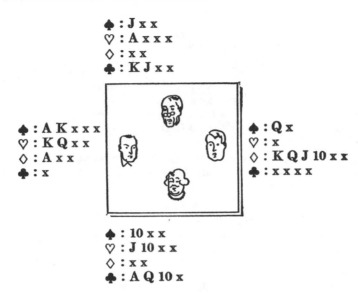

♠ : J x x
♡ : A x x x
◊ : x x
♣ : K J x x

♠ : A K x x x
♡ : K Q x x
◊ : A x x
♣ : x

♠ : Q x
♡ : x
◊ : K Q J 10 x x
♣ : x x x x

♠ : 10 x x
♡ : J 10 x x
◊ : x x
♣ : A Q 10 x

The Bidding

NORTH	EAST	SOUTH	WEST
Pass	Pass	Pass	1 ♠
Pass	2 ◊	Pass	2 ♡
Pass	3 ◊	Pass	4 ◊(a)
Pass	Pass (b)	Pass	

(a) So far in this rubber Mr. Smug has been bidding surprisingly well. In spite of partner's sign off his hand is worth another try.

(b) A typical example of Futile Willie's losing tactics. His hand is not very strong but the bidding shows that there must be a good chance of making five Diamonds. He does hold the Queen of Spades, which might be invaluable; his Diamonds are solid: and his partner, who has bid two suits and supported a third, is marked with a singleton Club. Five Diamonds is not a certainty, but there must be a play for it. And with a small slam safely tucked away and opponents still not vulnerable, the opportunity of clinching a nice rubber should not be missed.

However Futile Willie thinks differently.

[129]

The Play

```
                        N
                     ♠ : J x x
                     ♡ : A x x x
        W            ◇ : x x                    E
   ♠ : A K x x x   ♣ : K J x x        ♠ : Q x
   ♡ : K Q x x                        ♡ : x
   ◇ : A x x           S              ◇ : K Q J 10 x x
   ♣ : x            ♠ : 10 x x        ♣ : x x x x
                    ♡ : J 10 x x
                    ◇ : x x
                    ♣ : A Q 10 x
```

Mrs. Guggenheim led a trump. Willie won and led a Heart. The Unlucky Expert won and led a second trump. Six Diamonds were now made.

Points Chucked by East-West

700 for rubber, less 50 (value of part score). Total 650.

Total Chucks

North-South 970. East-West 650.

The Score Sheet

N—S	E—W
	100
	40
	500
═══	═══
	120
	80

Dealer East.　East-West vulnerable.

♠ : x x x
♡ : J 10 x x
◊ : x
♣ : A K x x x

♠ : J 10 x x x x
♡ : K Q x x x
◊ : None
♣ : Q x

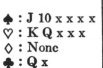

♠ : Q
♡ : 9
◊ : K Q J x x x x x
♣ : 10 x x

♠ : A K 9
♡ : A x x
◊ : A 10 9 x
♣ : J x x

The Bidding

EAST	SOUTH	WEST	NORTH
4 ◊ (a)	Dble.(b)	Pass	Pass
Pass			

(a) Nice going, Willie! On the previous hand where the worst that could happen to you was down one with a 100 honors, it was not worth chancing five Diamonds. But now, as dealer, with nothing known about the hand, vulnerable against non-vulnerable opponents, it is worth bidding four Diamonds on a probable seven playing tricks.

(b) Even Mrs. Guggenheim knows what to do here.

The Play

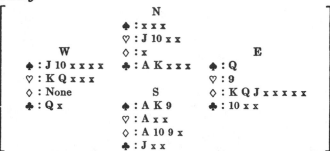

```
                        N
                   ♠ : x x x
                   ♡ : J 10 x x
        W          ◇ : x                    E
  ♠ : J 10 x x x x  ♣ : A K x x x    ♠ : Q
  ♡ : K Q x x x                      ♡ : 9
  ◇ : None              S            ◇ : K Q J x x x x x
  ♣ : Q x          ♠ : A K 9         ♣ : 10 x x
                   ♡ : A x x
                   ◇ : A 10 9 x
                   ♣ : J x x
```

The hand is foolproof. East can take six tricks and no more. Down 1100.

The Post Mortem

"Thank you, partner," says the Unlucky Expert with the first trace of a smile he has shown since the rubber started.

"Sorry, partner," says Futile Willie. "I had to bid it. I had nine Diamonds."

"Bad luck," says Mr. Smug, who can't count, but is at any rate a good loser. "I might have bid four Spades."

"I double that too," says Mrs. Guggenheim, still glowing under partner's unaccustomed praise.

"You had eight diamonds," says the Unlucky Expert, who *can* count.

Points Chucked by East-West

1100 less 400 (value of game available to opponents). Total 700.

Total Chucks

North-South 970. East-West 1350.

The Score

N—S	E—W
	100
	40
1100	500
═══	═══
	120
──	──
	80

Dealer South. East-West vulnerable.

♠ : J 9 x x x
♡ : K x x
◊ : Q 10 x x
♣ : x

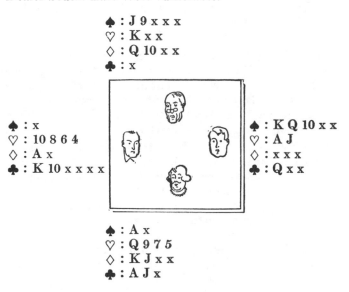

♠ : x
♡ : 10 8 6 4
◊ : A x
♣ : K 10 x x x x

♠ : K Q 10 x x
♡ : A J
◊ : x x x
♣ : Q x x

♠ : A x
♡ : Q 9 7 5
◊ : K J x x
♣ : A J x

The Bidding

SOUTH	WEST	NORTH	EAST
1 ♡(a)	Pass	1 ♠	Pass
1 N.T.(b)	Pass	2 ♡(c)	Pass
Pass(d)	Pass		

(a) In the good old days before the Strong No Trump was invented, Mrs. Guggenheim was in no trouble on this type of hand. She bid one No Trump and left the rest up to her partner, who usually took her out. But now the hand is not strong enough to bid a No Trump; and it is too strong to pass. Now she has three available bids open to her but she dislikes them all. Her natural impulse is to bid one Diamond. But she has been taught that when she holds two adjoining suits of the same length, she must bid the higher ranking suit first. Q, 9, x, x is not her idea of a suit; but she has been told by the experts that it is quite good enough. So if she doesn't bid it she will be wrong again. She might, of course, shelve the issue by bidding one Club, which the experts permit. But supposing she is left in with only three trumps! So with great reluctance she bids one Heart.

[133]

(b) Mrs. Guggenheim regrets that her partner has not bid Diamonds or Clubs. She could have supported either bid and been out of all her troubles. Now she supposes she ought to show her second suit, and bid two Diamonds, but that is really beyond her. Why, it's simply asking to be put back to two Hearts. So she bids one No Trump.

(c) The Unlucky Expert doesn't like this a bit. He never likes it when Mrs. Guggenheim has to play a hand. Is there any bid other than two Hearts that he *can* make? He might bid two Diamonds, or possibly re-bid his Spades, but there is no guarantee that Mrs. Guggenheim will not now bid two No Trump! He bids two Hearts.

(d) Poor Mrs. Guggenheim. In spite of all her efforts, here she is back in her Q, 9, x, x, suit. She considers bidding two No Trump; she knows her partner's bid is not strong, but after all she hasn't got such a bad hand and she has got such bad Hearts. She looks at her partner and abandons the idea. He would be so sarcastic. She passes.

This is a typical example of how the fear the Unlucky Expert inspires in his partners works against him. With a more pleasant partner, Mrs. Guggenheim would have followed her impulse and bid two No Trump. And North could now have bid three Diamonds, which Mrs. Guggenheim would have passed gratefully.

Three Diamonds is down one against perfect defense, but perfect defense is not necessarily bound to happen. And in any event a reasonably good player is likely to get a better result playing the hand at three Diamonds than Mrs. Guggenheim playing it at two Hearts.

The Play

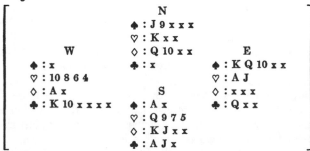

```
                        N
                   ♠ : J 9 x x x
                   ♡ : K x x
        W          ◊ : Q 10 x x          E
  ♠ : x            ♣ : x             ♠ : K Q 10 x x
  ♡ : 10 8 6 4                       ♡ : A J
  ◊ : A x               S           ◊ : x x x
  ♣ : K 10 x x x x  ♠ : A x         ♣ : Q x x
                   ♡ : Q 9 7 5
                   ◊ : K J x x
                   ♣ : A J x
```

Mr. Smug huddled and made another surprisingly good lead. With four trumps he decided he did not want to ruff and led a small Club. Really the man was playing above himself

[134]

Mrs. Guggenheim gazed at dummy and decided she must try to make as many tricks as possible as quickly as possible. She won the first trick with the Ace of Clubs and ruffed a Club, re-entered her hand with the Ace of Spades and ruffed another Club.

Four tricks already! Not so bad.

She now led a Diamond. West won with the Ace and led a trump. East won with the Ace and played the King of Spades. West discarded his losing Diamond. Well done, Mr. Smug.

East played the Queen of Spades. Mrs. Guggenheim sighed and discarded a Diamond. West discarded a Club.

East now played a Diamond and West ruffed.

The situation now was:

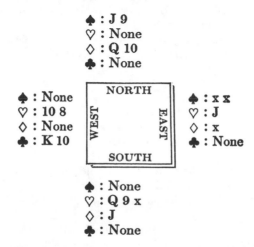

♠ : J 9
♡ : None
◇ : Q 10
♣ : None

♠ : None   NORTH   ♠ : x x
♡ : 10 8   ♡ : J
◇ : None   WEST   EAST   ◇ : x
♣ : K 10   ♣ : None
               SOUTH

♠ : None
♡ : Q 9 x
◇ : J
♣ : None

And East-West had won five tricks.

Mr. Smug now led the ten of Clubs; and Futile Willie, rising to the occasion, trumped with the Jack. Mrs. Guggenheim overtrumped with the Queen.

She now made a colossal effort and began to count trumps. One round had been played. That was four. She had ruffed twice in dummy—six. West had ruffed once—seven. East had ruffed and she had over-ruffed—nine. She had two, that meant there were only two trumps out. If they were divided and she played a trump she would only be one down, because she was practically certain her Diamond was good.

Of course, a complete count on the hand became available when East trumped the fourth Club, but Mrs. Guggenheim could not soar to such heights. Hoping for the best she played a trump.

Three down.

"Thank you, partner," said the Unlucky Expert without a smile.

But it was all his fault really, and others like him, for teaching Mrs. Guggenheim to bid weak four-card suits.

It is never easy to play a hand with inadequate trump holdings. And players, many degrees superior to Mrs. Guggenheim, who can at a pinch produce a squeeze play, flounder helplessly about without the slightest idea of how to handle them.

This hand is an excellent example.

Playing it myself, I should expect the result to vary between one down and making an overtrick, according to the distribution and the defense. Against the present opposition and actual distribution I should expect to make it more often than not.

Mrs. Guggenheim went down three.

The great majority of players would go down two.

For the great majority could not resist the lure of ruffing Clubs immediately.

The play of this type of hand is largely a matter of timing; and it is impossible to lay down any general rules. On some hands it is advisable to try and grab as many tricks as possible. On others, the opponents must be allowed to make the early running. What you do then is decided by what they have already done.

On this particular hand it is clear that to get anywhere near the contract tricks must be made in Diamonds. Therefore, before anything else is attempted the Diamond suit must be established.

So, having won the opening Club lead with the Ace, the King of Diamonds should be led at trick two. The Club ruffs can wait.

Now it is quite possible that West, having won the Ace of Diamonds, will attempt to stop you getting your ruffs and lead a trump. This would not be a bad play on his part: remember he does not know your trump holding. If that happens, East is almost bound to win with the Ace and play his Jack.

Your contract is now home.

You win with the King of Hearts in dummy, enter your own hand with the Ace of Spades, ruff a Club, re-enter your hand with a Diamond and play the Queen of Hearts. Your two winning Diamonds will force West to ruff and you make eight tricks, with three trumps, two Diamonds, two Aces, and a Club ruff.

Now suppose at trick three West does not lead a trump but instead leads his singleton Spade. Best defense now will defeat the contract. But you must still make seven tricks.

The play goes as follows:
Win with Ace of Spades. This makes two tricks you have to
their one. Ruff a Club. Return to your hand with a Diamond.
Ruff another Club.

You have now won five tricks to their one. You cannot afford
to play trump—your best course is to play another Diamond
and hope that the ruff will help you. West ruffs and the situation is as follows:

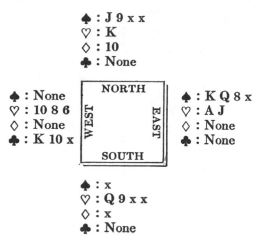

♠ : J 9 x x
♡ : K
◇ : 10
♣ : None

♠ : None
♡ : 10 8 6
◇ : None
♣ : K 10 x

NORTH

WEST   EAST

SOUTH

♠ : K Q 8 x
♡ : A J
◇ : None
♣ : None

♠ : x
♡ : Q 9 x x
◇ : x
♣ : None

West now leads a trump. East wins and plays the King of
Spades followed by the Queen of Spades. You ruff and West
over-ruffs. West leads a Club which East trumps with the Jack.
You overtrump and lead your last Diamond. West trumps and
your last trump makes. One down.

But that is perfect defense. It is always possible that East
will not trump the Club, arguing that, as it is the best Club anyway, why waste a trump? In that case your Queen of trumps
draws both outstanding trumps and you still make your contract.

I have gone into this hand in detail. It is the least sensational of all the hands in this rubber. But it is the sort of hand
which over a period of time costs you far more than the more
sensational swings.

Part score made. Or part score down two. It mounts up over
the year.

Chucks by North-South
Two Hearts, three down instead of one down. 100 points.

Total Chucks

North–South	East–West
1070	1450

The Score

N—S	E—W
	150
	100
	40
1100	500
==	==
	120
	80

DEAL NO. 5

Dealer West. East-West vulnerable.

♠ : x x
♡ : x
◇ : A K Q J x x
♣ : J 9 x x

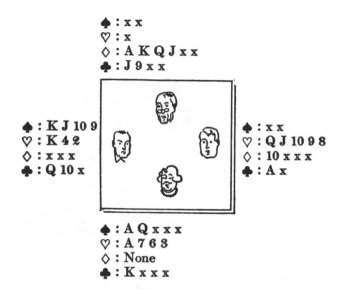

♠ : K J 10 9
♡ : K 4 2
◇ : x x x
♣ : Q 10 x

♠ : x x
♡ : Q J 10 9 8
◇ : 10 x x x
♣ : A x

♠ : A Q x x x
♡ : A 7 6 3
◇ : None
♣ : K x x x

The Bidding

WEST	NORTH	EAST	SOUTH
Pass	1 ◇(a)	Pass	1 ♠
Pass	2 ◇	Pass	2 ♡
Pass	2 N.T.(b)	Pass	3 N.T.(c)
Pass	Pass	Pass	

(a) Personally I agree with the Unlucky Expert in opening the bidding on his hand. The Diamond suit can be rebid safely many times; and, if a partner should get slam-minded in face of discouragement, then the hand is probably good enough to make it.

(b) A bad bid with a good partner—three Diamonds is correct. With Mrs. Guggenheim, however, the bid is pardonable for she is quite capable of bidding three No Trump over a three Diamonds sign off. So it's better to bid two No Trump. At least you play the hand yourself.

(c) Mrs. Guggenheim bids three No Trump thankfully.

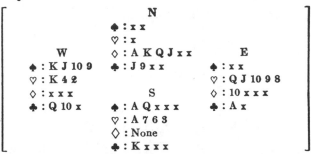

Futile Willie led the Queen of Hearts.

The Unlucky Expert inspected the dummy. The Diamond void was an unexpected and most disagreeable complication. Prospects looked hideous. Worse still, it was impossible to blame it on his partner. He could only be thankful he wasn't doubled.

However, there was nothing to be gained by ducking.

"Thank you, partner," he said gravely, and played the Ace of Hearts.

Mr. Smug fell from grace. He knew he should throw the King of Hearts, but he just couldn't bring himself to waste a big card like that. He compromised with the four of Hearts. This, of course, told his partner nothing.

Declarer led a small Club, Mr. Smug played low, Declarer with a confident air played the nine.

Futile Willie nonchalantly played low!

He had it all worked out. If he took the trick, he had argued, it left him with no entry to make his Hearts. On the other hand, if he ducked, declarer might be tempted to take the Spade finesse which would lose, and then his Hearts would be set up while he still had the Ace of Clubs.

This is typical Futile Willie reasoning, logical enough at first sight but sheer nonsense on further reflection. A sound enough play against a Mrs. Guggenheim, who is probably misplaying the hand, but a waste of time against a capable declarer.

Consider the situation from East's point of view and forget, for the moment, that you know the other three hands.

What conclusions can you reach?

First you are inclined to place North with the King of Hearts. It is not certain, for the two of Hearts is missing, but it is probable.

Secondly, either the declarer holds Q, J, 10, 9, of Clubs or the nine of Clubs is a finesse.

But, declarer is in no hurry to take the Spade finesse. For if that were the case, he would have won the first trick with the King of Hearts (which you think he holds) and taken the finesse right away. So it looks as if he is trying to knock out your entry.

Furthermore if his Clubs are Q, J, 10, 9 the Clubs will certainly be continued so there is no point in holding up the Ace.

But you ask, suppose the nine of Clubs was finessed from say Q, 10, 9. Might not declarer now abandon the suit believing East to hold A, J?

Yes, if the Declarer were Mrs. Guggenheim, she might. But a good declarer cannot hold Q, 10, 9. It is your entry he is trying to knock out, and in that case his correct play is the Queen of Clubs.

So you boil it down to the possibility that declarer's Clubs are Jack high. And at once the whole hand gets very suspicious. Why play that suit at all?

You now remember that declarer has bid and rebid Diamonds. You note the void in dummy and begin to get somewhere near the true situation.

Declarer is clearly desperate for entires.

He must bring in his Diamond suit in order to make his contract. He may be expecting to concede one trick in that suit before it can be set up—in which case he needs two entries into his own hand and he hasn't got them.

Or the Diamond suit may be solid, in which case he only needs one entry—*and he hasn't got it*. Which means he hasn't got the King of Hearts.

Partner played the four of Hearts. The two of Hearts is missing.

But whichever of these conjectures is the right one, it is now quite clear that the hold-up of the Ace of Clubs cannot gain and might very well lose.

A better player than Futile Willie would make this reasoning. A worse one would not get so far as Futile Willie and still play the Ace. And both of them would be right.

But Futile Willie ducked and the Unlucky Expert now made his contract with a Club, two Aces, and six Diamonds.

Do you begin to see now why Futile Willie loses so much? He can invent chucks beyond the scope of a poorer player.

Chucks by East-West

3 No Trump made by opponents instead of four down. 400 plus 200. Total 600.

Total Chucks

North-South	East-West
1070	2050

The Score

N—S	E—W
	150
	100
	40
1100	500
═══	═══
	120
	—
100	80
—	—

Dealer North. Both sides vulnerable.

♠ : 10 x x
♡ : x x
◇ : Q 10 9 8
♣ : Q J 10 9

♠ : A Q J 8 x x
♡ : A Q x x
◇ : x x
♣ : x

♠ : K 9 x
♡ : K x x
◇ : A J x x x
♣ : A x

♠ : x
♡ : J 10 9 8
◇ : K x
♣ : K x x x x x

The Bidding.

NORTH	EAST	SOUTH	WEST
Pass	1 ◇	Pass	2 ♠(a)
Pass	3 ♣(b)	Pass	4 ♠(c)
Pass	4 N.T.(d)	Pass	5 ♡(e)
Pass	6 ♠	Pass	Pass
Pass			

(a) I agree with Mr. Smug. Modern bidding is all for a beautiful approach bid of one Spade on his hand, forces being
reserved for slam hands. But personally, I am old-fashioned
enough to believe that a forcing overbid is forcing to game
only. If my hand is good enough for game in face of an
opening bid from my partner, I have got to jump the
bidding at some stage anyway and I would far rather get
it off my chest at once, and leave the subsequent strong
action, if any, to him.

(b) A very easy and a very obvious waiting bid.

(c) Having forced, West is safe in bidding four Spades; for,
unless partner takes further action, there is no slam in the
hand.

[143]

(*d*) Partner does take further action. He is not even in doubt. With his high cards opposite a forcing overbid (even though it is only forcing to game) the bid stands out. If West can show two Aces there must be an odds-on play for six in the hand.

(*e*) Showing two Aces.
Very nice simple and easy bidding. It has to be for Mr. Smug and Futile Willie to achieve it.

And now let us look at the complications that arise if West responds to 1 Diamond with a beautiful approach bid of one Spade.

East is in trouble at once. One No Trump is an underbid and so is two Spades. Two No Trump is a slight overbid and so is three Spades.

If he bids one No Trump the slam will certainly be missed; for all West can do now is to bid four Spades. This will leave West feeling he would like to bid a little more, but not at all certain that he can afford it.

If he bids two Spades the slam might be reached as follows: West three Hearts; East four Spades; West four No Trump; East five Hearts; West six Spades. But what a wealth of opportunity for going wrong.

If he bids two No Trump, or three Spades, West certainly gets slam conscious. But as against that East is now conscious of his overbid and inclined to back pedal. He may even be tempted into cheating in his response to four No Trump.

Earlier in the book I wrote that the scientists have to bid twice as well as ordinary players to achieve the same results.

See what I mean?

The Play

```
                      N
                 ♠ : 10 x x
                 ♡ : x x
        W        ◊ : Q 10 9 8          E
 ♠ : A Q J 8 x x  ♣ : Q J 10 9    ♠ : K 9 x
 ♡ : A Q x x                      ♡ : K x x
 ◊ : x x              S           ◊ : A J x x x
 ♣ : x            ♠ : x           ♣ : A x
                 ♡ : J 10 9 8
                 ◊ : K x
                 ♣ : K x x x x x
                    [144]
```

North led the Queen of Clubs. Declarer won in dummy and examined the situation.

For Mr. Smug, he worked it out remarkably well. He saw that if the trumps and the Hearts didn't break, he might go down one. Therefore, the Diamond suit had to be established for a discard.

Really well done.

Accordingly at trick two he played the Ace of Diamonds and followed it with another Diamond.

Mrs. Guggenheim won with the King of Diamonds, looked at her partner in agony, wondering if he wanted anything, and led the King of Clubs, heaving a sigh of despair when it was trumped.

Mr. Smug now played Ace of Spades, followed by small Spade, winning in dummy with the King.

"Not down yet," he said to his partner, as South showed out. Smug led another Diamond.

But South showed out again and Mr. Smug shook his head. "Still a chance," he announced. There was only one entry left in dummy, so the Diamonds could not be brought in. But then the Hearts might break.

But they didn't. Neither was there a squeeze.

And so the contract went down one.

The Post Mortem

Futile Willie, who is above everything a scientist, was very cross. He told his partner he didn't have a force. He ran through the gamut of nonsensical arguments about the beauties of approach bidding. Mr. Smug retorted strongly that it was a perfectly good slam bid and that three things had to be wrong not to make it.

Mrs. Guggenheim asked if her play of the King of Clubs was right. The Unlucky Expert nodded gravely.

Futile Willie now found a new line of attack. He pointed out that the contract should have been made. After ruffing the Club, he said, Declarer should enter dummy with the King of Hearts in order to ruff another Diamond. Then, when the Diamonds didn't break, he could see he would need extra entries. And he should take a chance and finesse the Nine of Spades on the second round of trumps.

Well done, Willie! A most ingenious play and only you could find it. Of course, if the trumps should happen to be divided two-two, you would have gone down in a contract that a baby could make. Still, that wouldn't be the first time.

All the same, Willie, there is another far less spectacular

[145]

play that can only fail if the Diamonds are divided five and one. Let the Unlucky Expert tell you:

"I think," drawls the Unlucky Expert, "that if declarer ducks the first Diamond, it is perhaps, shall I say, a slightly superior way of getting the extra entry."

I trust you did not need the Unlucky Expert to point out this line of play to you. But if you did, then remember it. For the occasions where you can gain a tempo by ducking the first round of a suit instead of winning it are very numerous.

Chucks by East-West.

750 slam, 500 rubber, 180 below line, 100 penalty. Total 1530.

Total Chucks

North-South	East-West
1070	3580

The Score

N—S	E—W
	150
	100
100	40
1100	500
====	====
	120

100	80
----	----

Dealer East. Both sides vulnerable.

♠ : None
♡ : A 10 x x x x
◇ : A 10 9 x x x x
♣ : None

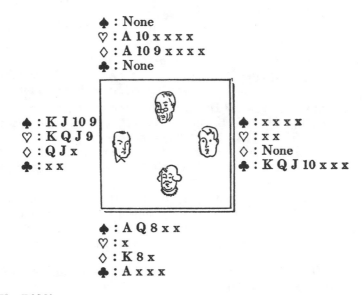

♠ : K J 10 9   ♠ : x x x x
♡ : K Q J 9   ♡ : x x
◇ : Q J x   ◇ : None
♣ : x x   ♣ : K Q J 10 x x x

♠ : A Q 8 x x
♡ : x
◇ : K 8 x
♣ : A x x x

The Bidding

EAST	SOUTH	WEST	NORTH
3 ♣(a)	3 ♠(b)	Dble.(c)	4 ♣(d)
Pass	Pass!(e)	Dble.!!(f)	Redble.(g)
Pass	Pass!!!(h)	Pass	

(a) In spite of the "success" of his earlier pre-empt, Futile Willie tries it again. He has, as usual, chosen the wrong type of hand for it. Pre-empts should be confined to hands which are useless except in their own suit and this is not the case here. It is admirably suited to a Spade contract, so that nothing should be done to discourage partner from bidding that suit. Even with the Spade suit divided as it is here, a Spade contract played by West will produce from eight to nine tricks, depending on the defense.

However, this time Futile Willie's luck is in.

(b) Eminently correct, though made in fear and trembling.

(c) Fatuous. With a weak three bid opposite there is no guarantee of defeating three Spades. And, for aught Mr. Smug knows, North might be about to bid four Spades.

[147]

But possibly with Mrs. Guggenheim due to play the hand, the temptation was too strong to resist.

(d) The correct book bid. As it combines a take-out of the Spade double with a slam try, it can only show a colossal red two-suiter. But, with his present partner, it is much more foolish than Mr. Smug's double of three Spades.

(e) What might have been expected. The mystified Mrs. Guggenheim passes. Incidentally, it is a moot point whether her correct bid here is four Diamonds, or five Diamonds.*

(f) Lunatic or genius? Did Mr. Smug foresee what was going to happen? Or did he think that his hand was so good that it would not pay to let their opponents play the hand undoubled in his partner's suit? Did he think he would gain more points by doubling whatever declaration they might now select.

(g) If the previous bids were foolish, this one is criminal. Mrs. Guggenheim has already shown that the proceedings are beyond her. What reason is there to suppose that this bid could achieve anything beyond deepening her mystification?

But it is very typical of the Unlucky Expert all the same. He'll do it again the next time.

(h) The only conclusion poor Mrs. Guggenheim could reach was that Futile Willie must have bid a psychic.

The Play

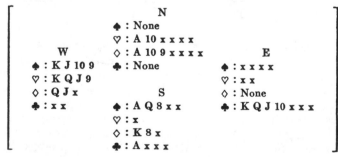

```
                        N
                    ♠ : None
                    ♡ : A 10 x x x x
        W           ◇ : A 10 9 x x x x        E
♠ : K J 10 9        ♣ : None           ♠ : x x x x
♡ : K Q J 9                            ♡ : x x
◇ : Q J x                  S           ◇ : None
♣ : x x             ♠ : A Q 8 x x      ♣ : K Q J 10 x x x
                    ♡ : x
                    ◇ : K 8 x
                    ♣ : A x x x
```

Futile Willie led the King of Clubs and the Unlucky Expert managed to make four tricks, one Club, one Spade, one Heart, and one Heart ruff. Down six redoubled—3400.

---

*Compare with hand discussed p. 56. From the angle of "how much worse might my hand be," it is quite a good hand. You have three cards headed by a high honor in one of the suits partner wants.

[148]

Incidentally, on careful play six Diamonds can be made. But five Diamonds is a reasonable par.

The Post Mortem

Some situations are too grim for words.

Points Chucked by North-South

3400, plus five Diamonds made, plus game, and rubber, 600 = 4000.

Total Chucks

North-South	East-West
5070	3583

The Score

N—S	E—W
	3400
	150
100	40
1100	500
═══	═══
	120
────	────
100	80
────	────

Dealer South. Both sides vulnerable.

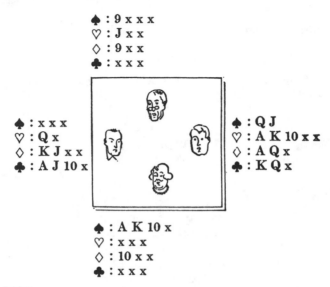

♠ : 9 x x x
♡ : J x x
◊ : 9 x x
♣ : x x x

♠ : x x x
♡ : Q x
◊ : K J x x
♣ : A J 10 x

♠ : Q J
♡ : A K 10 x x
◊ : A Q x
♣ : K Q x

♠ : A K 10 x
♡ : x x x
◊ : 10 x x
♣ : x x x

The Bidding

SOUTH	WEST	NORTH	EAST
Pass	Pass	Pass	1 ♡
Pass	2 ◊(*a*)	Pass	2 ♠!(*b*)
Pass	3 N.T.(*c*)	Pass	4 N.T.(*d*)
Pass	5 ◊(*e*)	Pass	6 N.T.(*f*)
Dble.(*g*)	Redble.(*h*)	Pass (*i*)	Pass
Pass			

(*a*) One of the few cases where I am in agreement with a response at the two level on a four-card suit. The hand has sufficient strength to bid two No Trump, but the weakness in Spades makes it advisable, if possible, for that declaration to be made by partner. Personally, I should bid two Clubs, as it is slightly the better suit and also offers partner the chance of bidding Diamonds. But there is little choice.

(*b*) Absolutely delightful. Futile Willie, of course, plays reverses as forcing, so he can see no harm in the bid. Bless him, he can see no harm in the bid!

To be quite fair, Willie's hand is a difficult one to bid. Now that partner has bid Diamonds, prospects are decidedly slammish but there is no entirely satisfactory

[150]

bid to make which can investigate this possibility without running the danger of taking the contract too high. If the hand contained one more Spade the best shot would be the slight underbid of three No Trump, which still leaves the hope that partner might find another bid. But as the hand contains Q, J, alone, three No Trump is not safe, and might go down whereas five Diamonds is cold.

As it is hard to visualize West with any hand which will not offer a play for five Diamonds, a possible bid is four No Trump immediately, with the intention of playing the hand at five Diamonds if West shows one Ace or no Aces: and at six No Trump if he shows two.

Another possibility is to explore the situation with a bid of three Clubs, taking the slight risk of partner passing. If he supports Clubs it can only mean that his Diamonds are good and the contract can be played in that suit. And if he bids No Trump you know at least that you have all four suits stopped.

But whatever the best bid, there is no argument at all that two Spades is easily the worst.

(c) Automatic. Partner holds Spades and Hearts, he holds Clubs and Diamonds, there is no apparent misfit, and the point count is more than ample.

(d) Futile Willie gets excited. What a rubber to win! With a slam! All his losses for the day back in one fell swoop. True, he has already shown a good hand by reversing; but not quite as good as he's actually got.

(e) Showing one Ace.

(f) It suddenly dawns on Willie that he doesn't know in what declaration he wants to play the contract! The Diamond suit has never been rebid. And when Willie remembers the sort of suit on which he himself might respond with two Diamonds, six Diamonds becomes much too dangerous. Why, partner might hold no better than 9, x, x, x! But by emphasizing to himself that Mr. Smug *has* bid three No Trump, and forgetting that he himself has bid Spades, he finds the solution.

(g) It took Mrs. Guggenheim a long time to find the double. Memories of previous unsuccessful doubles were still acute. So she had to consider very carefully what would happen if the enemy switched into seven Diamonds or seven Hearts. Eventually she decided that they could not make that either.

But, of course, she had forgotten that it was not her lead.

[151]

(h) Eminently correct on his partner's bidding.

(i) I regret that I cannot produce the intonation of resigned despair. But look at the Unlucky Expert's hand, consider what is known of Mrs. Guggenheim's judgment and defense, and, maybe, you can imagine it.

The Play

```
                        N
                  ♠ : 9 x x x
                  ♡ : J x x
          W       ◇ : 9 x x              E
  ♠ : x x x     ♣ : x x x        ♠ : Q J
  ♡ : Q x                        ♡ : A K 10 x x
  ◇ : K J x x          S         ◇ : A Q x
  ♣ : A J 10 x    ♠ : A K 10 x   ♣ : K Q x
                  ♡ : x x x
                  ◇ : 10 x x
                  ♣ : x x x
```

"My lead?" said Mrs. Guggenheim eagerly.
"Yes," said Futile Willie.
"No," said Mr. Smug.
They sorted it out.

And now the Unlucky Expert faced a ticklish problem. His partner's desire to lead had made it clear that the double was not a lead-directing double. (As though Mrs. Guggenheim would ever be capable of such a thing anyway!) Therefore, it could only mean she had the high card strength to defeat the contract and, as the opponents almost certainly held three Aces, it must be the Ace, King of one of the suits. But which suit? It was unlikely to be Hearts as he himself held the Jack and East had opened the bid with one Heart, and, therefore, unlikely merely to hold Queen high. It was certainly not Clubs as that suit had never been bid, and would therefore certainly be well covered by both sides to undertake a six N.T. contract. And it couldn't be Spades, for East had bid that suit, had no reason to to place his partner with any strength in it, and knew the lead would be coming through him.

Therefore, it was almost certainly Diamonds. Smug's Diamonds must be headed by Queen, Jack; and Mrs. Guggenheim, thinking it was her lead, had doubled on the Ace, King. That was cleary the explanation.

It took the Unlucky Expert very little time to work all this out. That was easy. But now he had another and far more ticklish problem to solve.

Would it be ethical to lead a Diamond?

There was no doubt that, technically, his partner's double was a lead-directing double, calling for a lead in one of the suits bid by dummy—either a Spade or a Heart. If Mrs. Guggenheim had not announced her mistake by her question about leading, he would have had to pick his lead between these two suits. And, on his holding of the Jack of Hearts, he would have picked a Spade.

Was it ethical to take advantage of illegally acquired knowledge of the situation?

Clearly it was not. The Unlucky Expert gritted his teeth. Far better to lose a few more thousand points than to imperil his reputation as an ethical player.

He led a Spade. Result: down three redoubled—1600 points.

The Post Mortem

Futile Willie and Mr. Smug had quite a nice wrangle trying to pin the blame on each other; while Mrs. Guggenheim, pink with pleasure, beamed her delight at the table.

But the Unlucky Expert sat in a daze throughout.

Could there be justice after all?

Points Chucked by East-West

1600, plus five Diamonds made (game and rubber), 600=2200.

Total Chucks

North-South	East-West
5070	5780

The Score.

N—S	E—W
	3400
1600	150
100	40
1100	500
===	===
	120
---	---
100	80
---	---

(Sympathizing with the sufferings of the Unlucky Expert, and feeling also that this rubber should contain at least one decently played hand, I have arranged for it to end with a classic example of a dummy reversal and squeeze that should keep him happy for weeks.)

This hand was actually played by my ex-team mate, J. C. H. Marx, many years ago. And he is just as good as all that.

The bidding, which couldn't matter less, has been altered to suit the present protagonists but the play remains as it was.

(I hasten to add that, save for their skill in dummy play, there is no other resemblance between Mr. Marx and the Unlucky Expert.)

Dealer West. Both sides vulnerable:

♠ : A Q x x
♡ : A Q 10 5 4 2
◇ : 10 8 x
♣ : None

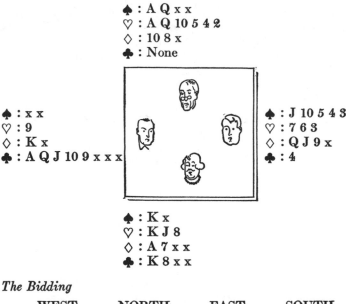

♠ : x x
♡ : 9
◇ : K x
♣ : A Q J 10 9 x x x

♠ : J 10 5 4 3
♡ : 7 6 3
◇ : Q J 9 x
♣ : 4

♠ : K x
♡ : K J 8
◇ : A 7 x x
♣ : K 8 x x

The Bidding

WEST	NORTH	EAST	SOUTH
5 ♣(a)	5 ♡(b)	Pass	6 ♡(c)
Pass	Pass	Pass	

(a) No half measures for Mr. Smug!

(b) Normally, the Unlucky Expert would never have taken such a risk, and Mr. Smug might well have been allowed to play the hand—possibly undoubled.

[154]

But under the succession of events the Unlucky Expert was no longer normal.

(c) Flushed with the success of her double on the previous hand, Mrs. Guggenheim finds a Master bid!

The Play

East led the four of Clubs. Dummy played low, West the nine, and declarer trumped with the two of Hearts.

I suggest, at this point, that you study the situation and see whether, even with all the four hands exposed, you can figure out how to make the contract.

There appear to be three losers in declarer's hand: one Spade and two Diamonds. The Spade can be ruffed in dummy, but the two Diamond losers appear inevitable. There seems no prospect of a squeeze because dummy's only menace card, the fourth Diamond, cannot be established without losing two tricks.

Hopeless?

That is because you have only considered the hand from the point of view of declarer's losers.

But now consider it from dummy's point of view. In other words, imagine that you, with dummy's hand, are playing the contract at six Hearts.

Now you have seven possible losers: four Clubs and three Diamonds. The four Clubs can be ruffed in dummy (this now contains no less than six trumps), and one Diamond can be thrown on the Queen of Spades. But dummy now contains a menace card in the fourth Spade. Provided West does not hold more than 3 Spades and two Diamonds, the squeeze on East is a certainty.

Did you find this line of play? If you did, you are above the average. Because it would never have occurred to the average declarer. The average declarer looks at the losers in his own hand and then looks to dummy to take care of as many of them as possible. He does not look at dummy and reverse the process. That is why he goes down on many hands which, had he been playing them with dummy's cards, he would have made easily.

It is only the first class players who are in the habit of viewing the combined holding as an entity and deciding each hand on its merits.

A very good habit if you can develop it.

Having discovered the dummy reversal, the Unlucky Expert proceeded to test the probability of the squeeze. He played a round of trumps winning in dummy with the Jack, and played a Club ruffing with the ten of Hearts. When East showed out,

West was placed with eight Clubs and one Heart. Prospects were now very hopeful.

However, there was still work to be done. Before the squeeze could operate, a trick had to be lost to get the timing right. As one Diamond trick has to be lost anyway, the declarer decided he might as well lose it at once. So at trick four he played a Diamond and ducked it into West's hand.

West won and did his best to break up the squeeze by returning a Diamond.

But it was no use. The Unlucky Expert, now full master of the situation, won in dummy with the Ace and led another Club. This was the position.

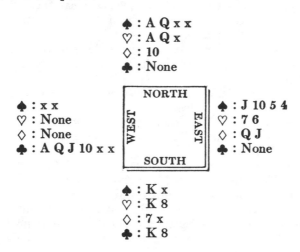

♠ : A Q x x
♡ : A Q x
◇ : 10
♣ : None

♠ : x x
♡ : None
◇ : None
♣ : A Q J 10 x x

NORTH
WEST   EAST
SOUTH

♠ : J 10 5 4
♡ : 7 6
◇ : Q J
♣ : None

♠ : K x
♡ : K 8
◇ : 7 x
♣ : K 8

Declarer ruffed the eight of Clubs with the Queen of Hearts. East discarded the Jack of Diamonds.

Declarer played his small Heart and won in dummy with the King. He led the King of Clubs and ruffed it with his Ace of Hearts.

East had to discard. Obviously he could not discard the last Diamond. If he discarded a Spade, declarer's Spades would be set up. He made a gallant attempt to avert the impending squeeze by under-ruffing with the seven of Hearts.

This left the situation as follows:

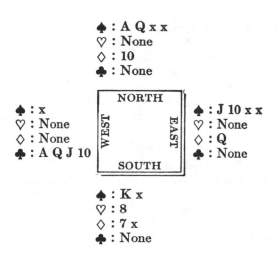

♠ : A Q x x
♡ : None
◇ : 10
♣ : None

♠ : x
♡ : None
◇ : None
♣ : A Q J 10

NORTH

WEST

EAST

SOUTH

♠ : J 10 x x
♡ : None
◇ : Q
♣ : None

♠ : K x
♡ : 8
◇ : 7 x
♣ : None

Declarer entered dummy with the King of Spades and played the eight of Hearts, throwing the ten of Diamonds from his own hand.

East gave up.

The Post Mortem

"I had to give it to you, hadn't I?" panted Mrs. Guggenheim triumphantly.

The Score

N—S	E—W
500	
750	3400
1600	150
100	40
1100	500
══	══
	120
──	──
100	80
	──
180	
──	──
4330	4200

Forty to North-South. A washout!

[157]

And now let us try an experiment.

Let us introduce into the table just one ordinary, sound, common-sense player. Let him be debarred from any brilliance; but equally let him abstain from any foolishness. Let him occupy each of the seats in turn.

And then, estimating the probabilities as fairly as possible, let us replay this rubber four times and see what happens.

FIRST

Replacing Futile Willie and sitting East.

Hand No. 1 is now played at five Diamonds and made. No argument about that.

Hand No. 2 is played at five Diamonds and made. Again no argument.

East-West win a 9-point rubber in two hands.

SECOND

Replacing Mr. Smug and sitting West.

No change for hands Nos. 1–4 for up to that point Mr. Smug has not made a mistake that matters.

On Hand No. 5 however three No Trump is defeated. On the opening lead the sound player throws his King of Hearts under the Ace and now, not even Futile Willie can fail to break the contract.

And on Hand No. 6 the sound player makes the small slam without difficulty.

Again East-West win a 14-point rubber from non-vulnerable opponents.

THIRD

Replacing the Unlucky Expert and sitting North.

On Hand No. 1 the sound player will not find the brilliant opening lead found by the Unlucky Expert. But, as the slam was still made in spite of it, there is no difference.

There is no difference also on Hands No. 2 to 6. On Hand No. 5, our sound player would certainly make the same play at tricks 1 and 2, and there is no reason to suppose Futile Willie would find a different defense.

Hand No. 7 however is more difficult to assess. But one thing is certain. A cue bid in opponent's suit is not a common-sense bid with Mrs. Guggenheim and our sound player would not dream of making it.

He would select one of his red suits. As Mrs. Guggenheim was likely to pass any bid he made the chances are he would select four Hearts as that, at any rate, will give him game.

[158]

Over four Hearts Mrs. Guggenheim will trance in agony and either pass, bid four Spades, or even achieve that beautiful monstrosity—a rescue bid of four No Trump.

But whatever she bids Mr. Smug is certain to double.

If Mrs. Guggenheim does in fact select the monstrosity of four No Trump, North now has the opportunity of making the brilliant inferential bid of six Diamonds.

But brilliance is barred. So we are content that North over West's double bids only five Diamonds.

Mr. Smug clearly doubles again and the contract is made comfortably. (We will not permit our sound player to play the hand well enough to make six.)

North-South win a 12-point rubber.

FOUR

Finally replacing Mrs. Guggenheim and sitting South.

On Hand No. 1 with the Unlucky Expert finding the same opening lead, and Mr. Smug making the same play, the slam is defeated.

As against that on Hand No. 2 Futile Willie will now bid and make five Diamonds, explaining that "it was worth a shot not vulnerable." That is the way his mind works.

Hand No. 3 shows no change.

Hand No. 4 is as before played in two Hearts. But with our sound player in control, and Futile Willie and Smug defending, two Hearts is made in comfort.

No. 5 is now played quietly in three Diamonds to make it game all. For with a part score the Unlucky Expert would bid three Diamonds on the third round and *South would pass.*

No. 6 shows no change.

No. 7 is once again more problematic for it is debatable whether Mr. Smug would double quite so freely with the sound player instead of Mrs. Guggenheim sitting South. But in any event North-South will reach the contract of five Diamonds, and may even reach six Diamonds.

Let us take it they bid and make five Diamonds undoubled.

North-South win a 20-point rubber.

Now that is interesting. One common-sense player, doing nothing out of the ordinary and refraining only from idiocies, wins this eventful rubber from all four positions, in between two and seven deals, for amounts ranging from nine to twenty points.

It just shows you how much is chucked by the average player in the course of a rubber.

And that concludes my views on why you lose at Bridge. You will approve of some of them, you will disagree hotly with others. That is as it should be. You will have lost most of the value of this book if you let yourself be overawed into accepting every word I have written as gospel.

It is my own gospel and it is right for me. It suits my type of game.

But you must play the type of game that suits you. You must not let yourself be hounded into something different, either by me or anybody else. Try and play your own type of game better, that is all.

If a "one Club" system suits you—stick to it. It will still be a filthy system, but if you like it, you will get your best results with it. For it is better to play a bad system well than a good system badly.

So take from this book only what helps you, what you have nodded approvingly over as you have read. Think about the rest by all means, but don't try to play it until you begin to feel that it may be right for you.